KEITH

SOLA
MYST
ERIUM

CELEBRATING THE
Beautiful Uncertainty
OF EVERYTHING

Copyright © 2022 by Keith Giles

First Edition

Cover design and layout by Rafael Polendo (polendo.net)
Cover illustration by BiroZsolt (shutterstock.com)

ISBN 978-1-957007-18-2

This volume is printed on acid free paper and meets ANSI Z39.48 standards.

Printed in the United States of America

 QUOIR

Published by Quoir
Oak Glen, California

www.quoir.com

DEDICATION

To Rafael Polendo, who believed in me when no other publisher would. I am forever grateful.

ACKNOWLEDGEMENTS

Thanks to everyone in the Square 3 online community for inspiring the conversations that sparked much of what I wrote about here, and to my wife Wendy for providing inspiration and feedback on this book in the earliest stages. Thanks also to Steve McVey, David Bentley Hart, Bishop Carlton Pearson, Gabriel Gordon, Jason Elam, Grant Morrison, Malcolm Gladwell, Carl Sagan, Carlo Rovelli, Anil Seth, Richard Rohr, Alan Watts, Charlie Kaufman, David Foster Wallace, J.J. Abrams, Adam Grant, Ricky Jay, Derren Brown, Carl Jung, Thich Nhat Hanh, and Black Elk.

AUTHOR'S NOTE

The title of this book is an intentional play on Martin Luther's Five "Solas" (Sola Scriptura, Sola Gratia, Sola Fide, etc.) from the Protestant Reformation. However, I am very aware that *Sola Mysterium* isn't correct Latin for "Only Mystery." As author and Bible scholar David Bentley Hart explained to me, "*Sola Mysterium* is gibberish ... You can't use a feminine adjective to modify a neuter noun ... If you wish a grammatically correct analogy of the former, you should write *Solum Mysterium* (or) *Solo Mysterio*."

After careful thought, I have decided to use the title found here simply because I likes the way it sounds. Please forgive my intentionally bad grammar.

TABLE OF CONTENTS

*"If our religion is based on salvation,
our chief emotions will be fear and trembling.
But if our religion is based on wonder,
our chief emotion will be gratitude."*

CARL JUNG

FOREWORD

When a man was once asked about his belief on a particular subject, his response was, "I believe what my church believes."

"Well, what does your church believe?" the other person continued.

"My church believes what I believe," he said.

"But what do you and your church believe?" the inquirer persisted.

"We believe the same thing," the man answered matter-of-factly.

Too many people are like that guy. They know what they believe for one simple reason: They've been told exactly what to believe and they have never really even examined or questioned it. Their belief system has been neatly arranged and kept in order for such a long time that the very thought of changing or adding to their defined dogma is literally out of the question. Their perspective is, "If it ain't broke, don't fix it."

This close-minded attitude is one of the greatest impediments to personal growth. Far from being wrong, questions are often bridges that lead to a deeper and wider understanding than we will ever have if we aren't willing to venture beyond the borders of beliefs that we currently hold. Questions can be an acknowledgment that we realize we don't know everything. To travel into the unfamiliar can be a journey into mystery and it is by embracing mystery that we open ourselves to new possibilities for growth.

In *Sola Mysterium*, Keith Giles leads us to courageously go places that many in the faith have never gone. While honoring the witness of Scripture, he takes us along the pathways of science and sociology and psychology and other disciplines to show us how to think about Reality in different ways. The result is that your imagination will be stimulated and your faith will be strengthened.

This book is brain candy on the one hand and pure nutrition for the soul on the other. It's a fun book to read and yet simultaneously challenges you to rethink things you've held sacred that may be short-sighted at best and simply wrong at the worst. It may make you doubt what you thought you've known and then turn right around and thrill you with new ideas that will immeasurably enrich you.

When Jesus was about to leave his disciples and return to the Father, He promised them that the Spirit of Truth would come. "He will guide you into all truth," Jesus told them. *All* truth. Not just religious truth. Not even just Bible truth. *All* truth.

That day has come and this book is an example of what Jesus was talking about. *Sola Mysterium* will guide you into truth that may be unfamiliar to you. You will find yourself telling friends about things you found fascinating in this book. It's the kind of book that will enlighten, encourage and even entertain you. Open your mind now and step into the space where Mystery abides.

STEVE MCVEY
Best-selling author of *Grace Walk*

SOLA MYSTERIUM

Please, do not tell me what you know about God.
Talk to me about all the things you do not know about God.

Rather than explain the unexplainable, try to imagine
All the wondrous beauty hidden
In the endless folds of eternity
That resides just outside of your certainty.

Our theology has remade God
Into a Book we can carry around
Or a symbol we can wear around your neck.

We have successfully reduced the Infinite
To fit on a sticker on the back of our car.

Oblivious to this blasphemy
Our capacity for awe neglected
Our lungs continually expand with Divine breath
Our hearts beat with the rhythm of Eternity
Our waking and sleeping, ebb and flow
Upon an ocean of exquisite Being.

Where is your uncertainty?
Where is your sense of wonder
In this universe of light and love?

Can you not hear the whispers within your own soul?
Can you not sense
The missing silence, deep
In the center of yourself?

Why would you remain here
In this senseless illusion
Even a moment longer?

Don't you long, even now
For every nerve to stand and resonate
With the glorious frequency of God?

Aren't you starving for that inner void of unknowing
To be filled with the perpetual flow of discovery?

There is a vast dimension of infinite wonder to be explored
Just beyond your senses.

The same Spirit that sustains you calls out to you
As deep unto deep

"Let go of this foolish certainty.
Embrace the truth that you
Know nothing of the One
Who knows you completely
Make room in your heart
For more than this.
There is a mystery that seeks to confound you.
There is a song you have never heard.
Quiet now.
Can you hear it?"

When you speak of all you know of God
– Which is nothing –
You speak more of yourself
Than of God.

But when you speak
Of all you do not know of God
– Which is everything –
You speak, at last
Of the One who transcends knowledge.

Yet, why speak at all?
Your words are empty.
Your wisdom is foolish.

You are not the rubric of God.
God is the rubric of you.

The secret of knowing the eternal Divine
Is not found by sitting at your feet.
You are found by sitting
In silence at the feet of the Divine.
There you find wisdom.
There you realize what is and what is not.

Begin without knowing. Know without beginning.

There is more of God to know
Than you will ever know in this lifetime.
Yet, you have barely begun to question.
The simple answers you were handed in your infancy
Have distracted you from the Beautiful Mystery.

The certainty you have built around yourself
Has shielded you from the joy of wonder.
The fear of the unknown has made you
Immune to curiosity.

Let go of your answers.
Question your certainties.
Launch out into the deep
Where all you have to hold on to is
The Love that holds on to you.

As long as our theology is about
Having the right answers
We will always miss the questions
That could lead us into
A deeper understanding
That transcends
Information and leads to ultimate
Transformation.

Do not speak to me of
All that you know of God.
What you know of God
Is as close to nothing
As it could possibly be.

Speak to me, and to your own soul
Of all that you have not yet known of God.
This is where true theology begins.

Questions are the answer.
Ask, and you will find.

Knock, and it will be opened.
Seek, and you will discover

There is more to know than you ever dreamed.
There is no wisdom to be found in speaking.

Listen.
Wait.
Receive.

INTRODUCTION

"The only true wisdom is in knowing that you know nothing."

SOCRATES

"What is fear? Nonacceptance of uncertainty. If we accept that uncertainty it becomes an adventure."

RUMI

Right off the bat I feel the need to confess something to you. It's not something I'm very proud of, but I think it's important to get this out there right from the very start.

To do this, I'll need to tell you a little story. It's about the day I was driving home in my car from work, talking to God, and expressing my concern that there wasn't really anything left for me to learn about the Bible, or Theology.

Seriously. I actually said these words out loud to God as I was driving down the freeway in Southern California at the ripe old age of 27: "There's really nothing about the Bible I don't already know the answers to," I sighed. "I feel like there really aren't any new things for me to learn when it comes to my faith."

Somewhere in Heaven there must have been an inaudible roar of laughter. But, I was dead serious. As a licensed and ordained minister, I had taught Bible Studies, preached from the pulpit, studied apologetics, read dozens of books on theology, taught seminars on Creation and Evolution at two different churches, led Sunday School programs for young adults and children alike, and basically, become the Bible Answer Man for anyone who was foolish enough to ask me a question about Christianity.

On one level, I was right. Sort of. I mean, I did have a lot of information. I had studied a lot about my faith. I had even studied philosophy and world religions at University. As far as I knew, I was an expert on theology and there was really nothing more for me to learn.

Sadly, once anyone reaches the point where they believe they already know everything, there really is nothing more you can teach them. Once you stop looking for answers, your brain stops learning and your curiosity dries up fast.

That's where I was that day in my car. My mind was closed. My ability to grow beyond that point in my life was frozen stiff. The cement had officially hardened.

So, what came next was not only a surprise to me, it was actually the most wonderful thing that could have possibly happened to me: *I lost the job I loved and became unemployed for over a year.*

Why was that so great? Well, to be honest, I really didn't think it was so great at the time. In fact, I was pretty sure it was the worst thing that had ever happened to me in my life up to that point. But, eventually, I began to see how this unexpected turn of events was actually the answer to that unintentional prayer I had spoken in my car that day.

Over the next year, I would struggle to find full-time work. Even though I had over 7 years of experience in the Christian Music Industry under my belt, knew dozens of people at some of the top record labels in the country, and interviewed for jobs that practically had my name on them, I could never find anything, no matter how hard I tried. During that time, I worked temporary jobs typing forms, answering phones, managing spreadsheets, updating warranty cards, and all sorts of other things, just to pay our bills and keep our two young boys fed and a roof over our heads.

That was honestly one of the most difficult and painful seasons of my entire life. It was humbling, and humiliating. I remember standing in line to fill up a grocery sack at the local food pantry. I remember praying on my knees for hours just begging God to give me a job, and turning in resume after resume, month after month, with no answers or job offers in sight.

But, if you want to know the truth, I wouldn't trade that experience in my life for anything in the world. Here's why: Because it was only during that painful, challenging, difficult season in my life that I learned something I could have never understood from a sermon, or a Bible study, or a theology book. What I learned during that time was simply this: *God saw me, and God loved me, and God was determined to provide for me and my family no matter what.*

Now, if you had asked me if I knew that God loved me, or that God was my provider a few years prior to this ordeal, I would certainly have said, "Yes, I know that." But, until I had to literally depend on God for my daily bread for more than a year, I really did not know that God loved me, or that God would provide for me in the same way. Before this experience, I might say that I knew the love of God was real, or that God was my source, but it wasn't until I had truly experienced those things in a tangible way that I really, truly *knew* that love and that provision in my bones.

So, it wasn't until a few years later that I remembered that conversation with God in my car that day. When I did, all of those experiences of God's love and provision, and daily care came flooding back to me. I laughed out loud. Because I could see, on the other side of that experience, just how little I really knew anything about God, or faith.

Suddenly, I had eyes to see just how little my understanding of God was based on my actual experience of God. Up to that point, everything I thought I knew about God was mere information on the page, or theories I had memorized to impress people around me. Until all I had left to hold on to was God, I really didn't know the God I was holding on to.

Why do you think I told God there was nothing more for me to learn that day in the car? Wasn't it obvious I had lost my sense of wonder? For me, every question had been answered. Every mystery had been solved. As far as I could see, there was nothing left to learn. But, of course, I couldn't have been more wrong.

My season of economic uncertainty helped to awaken me from my slumber. It opened my eyes to levels of faith that I had never even imagined were possible. It even showed me that the things I thought I knew so well were woefully incomplete. There were facets of God's love I had yet to understand. There were dimensions to God's character I had still not imagined. I knew God loved me because the Bible said so. But I didn't know just how much God loved me, nor what forms that love could take, until I was absolutely helpless to do anything other than cling to God's love with every ounce of strength in my body.

Now, I feel the need to stress something here before we continue: God did not cause me to lose my job. There were all sorts of factors in play that led me to that event and I do not believe that God was one of them. However, we do know that Jesus warned us that "in this life you will have trouble." So, trouble comes to everyone. We all have to go through hard times, no matter who we are, or how much faith we have, or how spiritual we may be. The Apostle Paul suffered. All of the Twelve Disciples suffered. The early Christian church suffered for over 300 years. Even our Lord Jesus suffered and died. Suffering is something we all must endure in this life. No one gets out alive, or unscathed. But, we do have this promise from God that says, "I will never leave you, nor forsake you." In other words, we may all go through the darkness, but we never go through that darkness alone. God is always at our side, weeping when we weep, suffering when we suffer, groaning when we groan and sharing that pain with the Father in words we cannot express.

So, God did not create my suffering. But, gladly, God certainly worked in and through my suffering to show me things I could never have seen otherwise. For that, I am so very grateful.

During that time of my life, a friend gave me a copy of a little book that became a lifeline for me and my wife. It was the book, "Let Go" by a guy named Fenelon. That book was like manna for our souls, to be honest. Every evening before bed, we would read a chapter together out loud and it felt as if it had been written just for us that very day. On one of those evenings, we read something that has never left me. In fact, I quote it all the time as a reminder to myself, and hopefully as an encouragement to others. It was this: *"If you stopped learning now, you wouldn't live long enough to put into practice all that you already know of Christ."*

This quote resonates with me on so many levels. First, it speaks to the need to stop thinking about my faith as the mere accumulation of information. The Gospel is not about acquiring knowledge that fills our brain. It's about encountering a God who fills our heart and transforms our soul from the inside out. Secondly, that quote reminds me to put what I know of Christ into practice. Because our faith is primarily about how we live, not what we know. Knowing is fine. It's obviously important. But, without the practice of our faith each day, that faith is worthless. Or, as James phrased it: *"Faith without works is dead."* And the thing I've learned about faith is that nothing kills it quicker than our sense of certainty. No, it's not our doubts or our questions about God that threaten our faith, it's our absolute conviction that we are already have God all figured out. The way some of us talk today, it's as if we've forgotten that God is a being beyond our comprehension. Instead, we have become convinced that we've got God in a box, or maybe bound in a Book, that is filled with answers that cannot ever be questioned.

But, deep down inside, even those who appear the most confident in their answers know the truth: God is bigger than our box, and God is beyond our Book, and the reality of God expands further than any answers we could ever put into words.

To know God is to know wonder. To experience God is to become acquainted with awe. To approach God, one must come emptyhanded.

It is our sense of curiosity that draws us closer to the Divine. It is our desire to know and be known that compels us to seek, and search, and inquire. That question mark buried deep within our soul is like a compass that points us towards the magnetic north where God dwells in unapproachable light, shrouded in mystery, covered in darkness, and yet we hear that still, small voice calling out to us, "Be still and know … " like the rise and fall of our own breath.

When we lose our sense of wonder, we lose our connection with the Divine. Once we become convinced—as I once was all those years ago—we find ourselves trapped in a prison of our own certainty where we foolishly believe we have answered every question and uncovered every mystery. But, of course, nothing could possibly be any further from the truth than this.

We cannot speak about God without admitting that what we are speaking of is something so far beyond our understanding, so inexpressible by our language, so incomprehensible by our minds, that to approach this concept accurately, we simply must do so with great humility and a sober sense of our own inability to fully grasp the great mystery that we call "God."

Of course, the real danger of becoming certain about God is that we inevitably end up creating a version of God in our minds that looks and behaves a lot like us. We construct a false image of the Divine that hates the same people we hate and affirms everything we already are. This is not the real God. It's the one we invent out of thin air. As Henri Rousseau famously observed, "God created man in His own image and then man returned the favor." This is why the illusion of certainty is so dangerous and why admitting the truth—that God is beyond our comprehension—is where true theology begins.

My hope in this book is to help us regain our sense of wonder again. To find joy in the everyday things. To experience a healthy dose of awe as we go through our day. To become curious once more about the incomprehensibly beautiful world we live in, and the endlessly fascinating Creator who takes great delight in our childlike curiosity.

This book is not about finding answers. If anything, I hope to whet your appetite for better questions that lead you down the rabbit hole to even better questions that you've probably never even considered before.

Where we're going there is no road. There is no map. There are no rest areas. This will be our journey into the unknown. To travel this road, we may need to let go of our assumptions. We may need to hold loosely to those things we thought we knew for certain. In fact, if we're not willing to have all of those things stripped away, we may never really make it all the way.

If you're convinced there is nothing more for you to know about God, or life, or the world around you, then maybe this isn't the book for you. But, if you're ready to entertain the possibility that there is more to know than you could ever imagine—then maybe, just maybe—you're ready to embrace this beautiful mystery and start pulling away the curtain to discover all the marvelous things you *don't* know.

I don't know about you, but I can't wait to get started.

Here we go.

Chapter 1

LISTEN CAREFULLY

*"Learning is the only thing the mind never
exhausts, never fears and never regrets."*

LEONARDO DA VINCI

*"Being listened to is so close to being loved that
most people can't tell the difference."*

DAVID OXBERG

Back when our boys were in elementary school, my wife Wendy and I used to take them to visit the residents of the Tustin Hacienda Senior Care Home in Tustin, California. We were usually visiting as part of our monthly outreach with our Kids Rock students at the Church we had helped to start that met just up the street.

Our usual routine was to gather all the seniors in the large community room around 2 p.m. for a song service, and then the parents would take their kids around the room to visit with the residents for a few hours. The conversation time was what the seniors there loved most. I'll never forget one dear woman who took my hand and pulled me down close enough for her to whisper to me, "The singing is okay, but we don't need it. Just keep bringing the children around so we can see their sweet faces."

For those seniors who were too frail to get out of their rooms, we would make our rounds to pray over them, or just sit and listen to them talk to us about their day or share stories about their lives growing up.

We all had our favorites. Alvin had a wide smile and a huge white beard that made him look like Santa. He loved to tell us stories about when he was a cook for General Patton's soldiers during World War 2; cooking enough chili for 200 men while bullets and mortars went off all around him. Roger loved to talk about his years working for the C.I.A., and how he was one of the architects of the contingency plan for evacuating essential personnel in the event of a nuclear attack. Dorothy was in a wheelchair and had a rare disease that made it hard for her to use her hands, and she had no fingerprints. She loved talking about her daughters and grandchildren with us.

What all of those beautiful people taught us was the importance of listening to one another. Our expression of love was to simply pay attention to each of them for a few minutes and share the joy, the wonder, the pain, and the beauty of the life they had once lived. It made them feel seen. It made the feel alive. It made them feel loved.

My friend Thomas Crisp taught me a lot about the ministry of listening. He used to get up early on a Sunday morning, put on a pair of old jeans and a t-shirt and drive over to the Dorothy Day House in Santa Ana, California. What he liked to do was to stand in line with all the other people who were there for the free breakfast so he could sit at a table with them and just listen to their stories. He didn't try to fix anyone. He never offered unsolicited spiritual advice. He simply sat down, ate his lukewarm eggs, and learned how to listen to the people most of us never even take the time to look in the eye.

Isn't it fascinating how listening to someone can be an expression of love? How being still, and quiet can open us up to receive someone's story? How our connection with other people begins with an expression of genuine curiosity about who they are, or what they think, or how they feel?

This is why I believe it's so important for us to come to God like this. To be still. To listen. To express genuine curiosity about a God who loves us more than we can possibly imagine, or comprehend. What better way to express our love for God than to sit quietly in God's presence and simply listen?

After all, doesn't a Being beyond our imagination deserve our curiosity? Isn't silence the appropriate response to someone so unimaginably grand? How could we even consider coming into the presence of anyone so endlessly fascinating with anything but awe in our hearts?

If listening to someone is equated with loving them, then might I suggest that—if we want to know God better—we should listen to God? If we want to experience more of God, we could begin by slowing down, taking a deep breath or two, and simply taking time to love God with our listening.

We can even show our love for God by the way we show our love for others: by listening. If we listen to others, we are loving them, and, at the very same time, we are loving God, too.

Have you ever tried this? Have you ever found a quiet place, turned off your phone, focused on your breathing, and just spent an hour or so in silence?

When we are quiet, wisdom floods into the empty space. When we simply rest in God's presence, our spirit begins to resonate at the frequency of the Divine. When we stop talking, stop asking, stop complaining, stop trying to find the answers; that's when we come to the beginning of wisdom; when we realize that God is right here, and has always been here, and will never leave us; never forsake us.

I love the way Alan Watts describes the wisdom that we can experience when we simply sit quietly and breathe:

> "You wait. You watch, and all that you see is what is happening of itself. You are breathing. The wind is blowing. The trees are waving. Your blood is circulating. Your nerves are tingling. It's all going on by itself. But, you know, that's you. That's the real you. The you that goes on of itself … it's you that is happening as when you breathe. Yes, you can get the feeling that 'I am breathing' by shoving your breath. But your breath goes on, day in and day out, without you ever doing anything about it, or even thinking of it. The same way your brain is functioning without you forcing it. So … this is the moment of which it is said man's extremity becomes God's opportunity. Because we have to stop. And when we stop we find a world that is happening rather than being done … and that happening, as distinct from doing, is our fundamental self … and our fundamental self is not just inside the skin. It's everything around us with which we connect."[1]

Connection is a very strong theme that I hope to develop throughout this book. Connection with God. Connection with others. Connection with our true selves. This is something many of us have lost touch with. We no longer feel a genuine connection with God because we've spent so much time going to church, or serving in the ministry, or running the endless hamster wheel of quiet time and morning devotionals and Bible studies, and daily journaling, and so many other religious activities. Ironically, these things may only end up making us feel exhausted trying to check all the boxes, or make us feel guilty for failing to keep the pace with these unrealistic expectations, all of which are grounded in doing more rather than

---

1   From "Ego Death Will Save The World", Alan Watts:
    https://www.youtube.com/watch?v=IdEA5zc-zIU

slowing down and breathing deep the breath of God which is all around us, all the time.

All of our religious striving only ends up making us feel farther away from God, not truly connected to God in a real, intimate way. So, maybe the problem is that we've understood "knowing God" the wrong way? Maybe it's not about filling our minds with information, or scheduling endless activities that demand every waking moment of our attention. Maybe there's a much simpler, more natural way of connecting with God?

Let's explore that more in our next chapter, shall we?

Chapter 2

RETHINKING
HOW WE KNOW

*"We are closer to God when we are asking questions
than when we think we have the answers."*

ABRAHAM JOSHUA HESCHEL

Before we can embrace mystery, we must first embrace the truth, which is that, when it comes to God, we know almost nothing about God.

We believe. We hope. We think. We are possibly even convinced. But none of us can really say we know anything for certain about the One who is the ground of all Being, the Source of all Life, the Spring of Eternal Wisdom, and the Infinity without beginning, or end.

If our primary understanding of God is measured in quantity of information, we must confess that our information is vastly limited. Our finite minds cannot fully comprehend an infinite reality. We can try. We can use analogies, even mathematical equations, to express the concept of something without end or beginning, but none of us can fully grasp such things with any sense of complete understanding.

But what if there is another way of knowing? What if there is a slightly different way of approaching our knowledge of God without falling into the trap of defining the undefinable with our woefully inept terminology and theology?

Jesus suggests that this is exactly what we must do if we are to ever begin this process of knowing God properly. He says that our knowledge of God must be closer to how a husband knows his wife through the intimate experience of lovemaking. Scandalous, but nevertheless true, this is what Jesus means when he says:

> "Now this is eternal life, that they would *know* you [God] and your son whom you have sent." (John 17:3, emphasis mine)

The word translated as "know" here is the Greek word *"ginosko"* which speaks of the sort of "knowing" that we see expressed in the intimacy shared between a husband and a wife during sexual intercourse. It's not the Greek word "episteme" which would suggest "knowing" in terms of having the right information about something.

As New Testament Greek scholar David Bentley Hart explains,

> "Gnosis [the root of "ginosko"] and episteme were always conceived of as two distinct modes of knowledge. The former meant knowledge by acquaintance (rather like the French connaître) and the latter knowledge about (rather like the French savoir). That is why the former [ginosko] could be used as a term for sexual intercourse."[2]

So, what Jesus reveals to us here is that knowing God is less like having all the answers to the questions, and more like an intimate connection with another person that conceives new life within us.

This means we need to learn how to shift our perspective from knowing God informationally to know God experientially. This requires us to become open to encounters with the Divine that inspire

---

2 From a personal email correspondence, Monday, 12/27/21 at 11:57 a.m.

ecstasy and defy mere explanation. This, my friends, is where real theology begins.

Once we move away from knowing God through information, we can begin to see why dividing over issues of theology is so foolish, and destructive. Because the faith we've inherited is one that is less about accurately explaining our various beliefs and more like an intimate encounter with a mysterious lover we can barely put into words, and perhaps even wonder if we should even try.

Rather than go down the rabbit hole to understand *how* our faith became more about information than transformation, let's just simply begin to focus our energies and efforts into learning to practice the sort of faith that is abandoned to the wonder and exquisite mystery of Divine experience.

Let's remember: God invented sex. It's not dirty. It's not evil. It is a tangible metaphor for God's desire to know us in the deepest possible way.

God is the one who uses the metaphors of Bridegroom and Bride to describe our relationship. God's love for us is as infinite and eternal as God's own nature, which is love.

Not only this, but our identity is rooted in this same love. We were created in the image of God. Love is who God is. Or, as one New Testament author phrased it:

"God is love, and all who live in love live in God, and God lives in them." (1 John 4:16)

So, imagine drawing near to God the way you would approach your lover. Imagine a spiritual encounter with God that left you as breathless as a first kiss. Imagine knowing God spiritually the same way you have known someone physically. What would that be like? How would you even begin?

This is the sort of theology God wants us to engage in. This is the kind of knowing we are invited to explore. Not the study of doctrines. Not the defense of our faith, but the scandalous intimacy of lovers in the hushed silence of a marriage bed on honeymoon night.

Once we understand that loving God is where everything begins, we can also begin to realize that loving others is also how we can experience the presence of God in other people.

"By this everyone will know that you are my disciples: if you love one another" (Jesus in John 13:35)

Simply put, the very best expression of true theology is love. But this can only happen if learn to loosen our grip on certainty and tighten our grip on exploring the implications of loving—God and others—without fear.

If we can successfully shift our perspectives about theology from information over to transformation, this allows us to prioritize what we know of God from our personal experience rather than from a systematic theology book, or a Sunday morning sermon.

To do this, we'll need to hold a bit more loosely to our certainties. We'll have to let go of our need to debate who's right or wrong. We'll need to become better lovers of God than we are keepers of inerrancy.

Information is about accuracy. Transformation is about growth. Information is about being right. Transformation is about being Christlike.

These are two very different ways of being, and behaving, aren't they?

Sometimes we might be tempted to believe we can do both of these things at the same time. But, in my experience, we are either focused on being lovers of Jesus, or we become focused on defining Jesus. One is about religion and the other is about practice. One is dedicated to defending our Orthodoxy, and the other is more concerned with incarnating something that transcends doctrine.

A good analogy might be that we cannot hold on to caterpillar ways of living and thinking once we've undergone the transformation to become butterflies.

How can we do this? What are the real barriers to shifting our perspectives away from faith as information towards faith as transformation?

That's what we'll explore in our next chapter.

Chapter 3

DECONSTRUCTING OUR
NEED TO BE RIGHT

*"The funny thing about my worldview is: no matter
how many times it changes, I'm always right!"*

JOSHUA LAWSON

I love this quote above for so many reasons. First, because it's from
my friend, Josh, but also because it's just so true. My views on several
things have changed over the last few years. Each time, however, I
have merely shifted my perspective and maintained my convictions
that I am right.

The other reason I love this quote is that it underscores our
tendency to always want to be right and to prove others wrong. This
is why, in a Christianity where the gospel is about having the right
information about God, the greatest heresy is to be wrong. It's also
why it's so easy for us to separate ourselves from people who hold
different beliefs than our own: because if they are "wrong"—or if
they disagree with us—that means they're heretical and that gives
us permission to break fellowship with them. Because, under these
assumptions, our agreement is the basis for our unity, not love.

It's like what comedian George Carlin once observed about how
we perceive people on the freeway. As he puts it:

"Have you ever noticed how everyone driving faster than you is insane and everyone driving slower than you is an idiot?"

This is where American Christianity is at today. Anyone less progressive than we are is insane and anyone more progressive than we are is an idiot. We've somehow made ourselves the standard for what is "normal" or "true" and if anyone is not in agreement with us, they must be stupid or deceived.

But there is another way to think about this quote above that I feel we might need to learn to embrace. Yes, every time my worldview changes, I can say I'm right, but this also means that I have been wrong before, and I am probably wrong about a few things right now, and I can rest assured that I will be wrong again in the future.

If we can learn to take this perspective, then we might develop a better sense of humility around our beliefs. Especially if we acknowledge that our beliefs have a tendency to shift, and we admit that our capacity for getting it wrong is infinite in scope.

This way of thinking should also lead us to have more grace for one another—especially when we encounter someone who believes now that we used to believe a few years ago.

This is the very reason why I often counsel people who are going through the process of spiritual deconstruction to also consider deconstructing their need to be right. Because, as Richard Rohr has said, "God is always bigger than the boxes we build for God, so we should not waste too much time protecting our boxes."

In other words, let's try to learn how to hold loosely to our beliefs. Perhaps even consider the possibility that our identity is separate from our beliefs, because we are not what we believe. Who we are remains the same, even if what we believe changes.

So, if we resist the temptation to allow the cement to dry; if we can maintain a loose grip on our certainty and learn to embrace the mystery of faith, I believe we will be better off in the long run.

As my friend Kenneth Tanner recently posted:

> "If you would be a theologian or pursue any kind of wisdom, get comfortable saying these sentences: I don't know. It's complicated. I was wrong. … I just haven't sat with it long enough to help you. I do not have the words to describe what I am seeing. Let me think about that … "[3]

When it comes to theology, one thing I believe should bring us great joy and excitement is the realization that there is more of Christ to know than any of us could ever imagine. God is greater than our imaginations. God is bigger than our thoughts. God is more wonderful than we could ever comprehend. God is beyond definition, description, explanation or understanding, and yet God is never beyond our ability to know. Why? Because knowing God is more about experience, connection and intimacy and less about information, facts or data.

If we look at the way Jesus taught his disciples, we'll see evidence of the way God entices us to engage our curiosity without offering a set of doctrines about certainty.

Jesus primarily spoke to people by telling parables or stories. In all of the Gospels, Jesus only ever explained one of those parables. All of the rest are left open for us to ponder, question and wrestle with the various possible meanings.

This is a strange way to communicate precise theological details, isn't it? In fact, it's the *worst possible way* I can imagine if your goal is

---

3   From Kenneth Tanner's Facebook post, 8/4/2021

to share unquestionable doctrines with your followers. However, it is the *best and most wonderful method possible* if your goal is to provoke imaginations, inspire curiosity, and engage the minds of people who seek to pursue the profound mystery of an infinite God.

This, I believe, is why Jesus told us, "Unless you change and become like little children, you will never enter the Kingdom of God." (Matt. 18:3) This may sound harsh, but it's not an arbitrary prohibition or rule. It's more like saying, *"If you want to be a lifeguard, you have to learn to swim,"* because, unless we can recapture our sense of childlike wonder and curiosity, we will never move beyond our reliance on theological certainty, and that certainty is the direct opposite of what it means to have faith.

Anyone who has children, or who remembers what it was like to be a child, knows that one thing children do constantly is ask questions. The questions "Why?" and "How?" and "What?" are almost never satisfied by any answers an adult can offer. Curiosity and wonder are the default setting in children. This is what Jesus encourages us to return to as adults who seek his Kingdom.

Therefore, as Eastern Orthodox Bishop, Kallistos Ware reminds us,

" ... it is not the task of Christianity to provide easy answers to every question, but to make us progressively aware of a mystery. God is not so much the object of our knowledge as the cause of our wonder."

If there's any crisis in our faith systems today, it is our lack of wonder. Certainty and dogmatism permeate our Christian institutions to the very core. It is as if the Infinite God of wonder has been defined, measured, mapped, profiled, and fully explored by those outrageously finite creatures we call theologians.

No, we do not lack for certainty today. Our lack is in this area of childlike curiosity. Where is our humble search for the endlessly beautiful, vast, and eternally-unknowable One whose name is too wonderful for words?

What makes our certainty about theology even more ridiculous is that Jesus himself told us that there was more truth for us to discover than what he gave us, and that this truth would come to us from different sources:

> "I have much more to say to you, more than you can now bear. But when he, the Spirit of truth, comes, he will guide you into all the truth. He will not speak on his own; he will speak only what he hears, and he will tell you what is yet to come." (John 16:12-13)

In other words, there is more of Christ to know than we have come to know. Not only this, but in the same Gospel, we are told that the scriptures themselves are an incomplete picture of everything Jesus ever said or did:

> "Jesus did many other things as well. If every one of them were written down, I suppose that even the whole world would not have room for the books that would be written." (John 21:25)

So, there is more truth for us to learn than what we can find in the Bible. The same Spirit of Christ which lived in Jesus will continue to reveal truth and speak to us long after the physical person of Jesus is gone.

One of the ways we see this being fulfilled was, of course, in the outpouring of the Holy Spirit at Pentecost when God poured out His Spirit on all flesh, both men and women, young and old, Jew and Gentile (See Acts 2). It was also fulfilled as people began to listen to the Holy Spirit and write what we now refer to as the New Testament scriptures. But it is also continually fulfilled within each and every one of us because, as those same scriptures contend, "We have the mind of Christ" (1 Cor. 2:16), and "You have an anointing from the Holy One and all of you know the truth" (1 John 2:20), and " ... the anointing you have received from God remains in you and you do not need anyone to teach you. But as his anointing teaches you about all things, and as that anointing is real, not counterfeit—just as it has taught you, remain in Him." (1 John 2:27)

Let me remind you that this word "anointing" is the same as the one used to signify that Jesus was the Christ (literally, "the anointed one"), and that we are "filled with the fullness of Him [Christ] who fills everything in every way," (Eph.1:23) And, "the same power that raised Christ from the dead is alive in you." (Rom. 8:11)

We are the incarnation of Christ in the world today. This means we can accurately and literally say, *"If you have seen me you have seen the Father, and Christ."* Why? Because Christ has come and made his home within me. Christ abides in me, and I abide in Christ. I have the mind of Christ, and I am made alive in Christ.

Paul calls this the great mystery of Christ in us, the hope of glory. And this hope is fulfilled as we awaken to this glorious reality and walk in this great mystery of Christ—who comes alive in us the more we come alive in Christ.

When Jesus tells us that there is more truth to experience than what he spoke to us in the Gospels, and that this truth would come to us through the Holy Spirit, which was poured out on all flesh, I believe he was also letting us know that more truth would come to us from other people, and other voices, from outside our religious systems and culture.

In other words, all truth is God's truth. When Jesus says the Spirit will lead us into all truth, he also adds this:

"He [the Spirit] will glorify me because it is from me that he will receive what he will make known to you. All that belongs to the Father is mine. That is why I said the Spirit will receive from me what he will make known to you." (John 16:14-15)

So, whenever we encounter truth from another source, we can rest assured that it is coming from the same Spirit, the same Christ, that Jesus received.

Now, I know that this makes some of us very nervous. This is something we have been warned against from the pulpit; the idea that there is "more truth" or "new teaching" from sources outside of Christianity is labeled dangerous. We've been told that anything outside of the Bible, or the Christian faith is heretical, and possibly even demonic in origin. But, that way of thinking seems to contradict what Jesus says to us in John 16, doesn't it? If Jesus tells us there is more truth to experience than what he told us, and if the New Testament declares that God's Spirit has been poured out on all flesh, and if we encounter truth from other people outside of our faith community, then why wouldn't we accept this truth as coming from Christ as Jesus said?

Of course, this doesn't mean we just accept any message we encounter. Not everything is Christlike. Not every teacher is true. Not every teaching is beneficial. This means we have to use discernment—and our own God-given mind of Christ—to determine what to accept and what to reject. But, how do we do that?

Here are a couple of ways we can know what is God-breathed and what is not. First, we can turn to 2 Timothy 3:16-17, a set of verses that are, ironically, quite often misused to teach that we should only find truth in the Bible. The verse, as it is rendered in most English translations says:

> "All Scripture is God–breathed and is useful for teaching, rebuking, correcting and training in righteousness, so that the servant of God may be thoroughly equipped for every good work."

The problem with interpreting this verse in this way is simply this: The Greek word for "Scripture" does not actually appear in the text.

That's right. Someone added the word "Scripture" here where it does not belong. The word found here is actually the word "graphia" which is the common term for "writings."

In other words, the verse actually says this:

"All the God-breathed writings are useful for teaching, rebuking, correcting and training in righteousness, so that the servant of God may be thoroughly equipped for every good work."

This means any writings that are useful for teaching, rebuking, correcting and training in righteousness are God-breathed writings. Which is why the Apostle Paul could quote pagan poets and prophets to idol-worshipping Gentiles in Athens to teach them about the "Unknown God" who loves them, provides for them, and is their Heavenly Father; the One in whom they all live and move and have their being (See Acts 17:28).

So, when we encounter truth in other writings, or other teachings, or even in other people, we can discern whether or not what we hear is true, or *God-breathed* by asking ourselves: *"Is this useful for teaching, correcting and training in righteousness?"* or *"Is this teaching Christlike?"* If they answer is "Yes", then we can receive it as being of the same Spirit as Christ told us these truths would come. If not, we can safely reject it and turn away.

But, do we encounter the same Christlike truths in other religions or from other sources outside of the Bible? I'll let you decide.

- **Buddha**: "Consider others as yourself." (Dhammapada 10:1)

- **Jesus**: "Do to others as you would have them do to you." (Luke 6:31)

- **Buddha**: "If anyone should give you a blow with his hand, with a stick, or with a knife, you should abandon any desires and utter no evil words." (Majjhima Nikaya 21:6)

- **Jesus**: "If anyone strikes you on the cheek, offer the other also." (Luke 6:29)

- **Buddha**: "If you do not tend to one another, then who is there to tend you? Whoever would tend me, he should tend the sick." (Vinaya, Mahavagga 8:26.3)

- **Jesus**: "Truly I tell you, just as you did not do it to one of the least of these, you did not do it to me." (Matthew 25:45)

- **Buddha**: "Abandoning the taking of life, the ascetic Gautama dwells refraining from taking life, without stick or sword." (Digha Nikaya 1:1.8)[4]

- **Jesus**: "Put your sword back into its place; for all those who take the sword will perish by the sword." (Matthew 26:52)

We might also consider the wisdom found in other voices outside our religious tradition, such as the great Native American shaman, Black Elk:

"The Holy Land is everywhere."[5]

This is exactly what God said to Jacob in his dream of the ladder to heaven: "I am with you and will watch over you wherever you go … " (Gen. 28:15). Meaning, the "Holy Ground" Jacob walked on

---

4   As quoted in *Jesus and Buddha: The Parallel Sayings,* edited by Marcus Borg, published by Ulysses Press.

5   From *Black Elk Speaks* by John G. Neihardt.

wasn't merely that place where he had the dream, but anywhere and everywhere he set his face to go.

When the Gospels speak of the veil in the Temple being torn in half at the crucifixion of Jesus, it speaks to this same idea that the Holy Presence of God is not hidden away, but is now unleashed upon everyone, everywhere.

This is also what is meant when it says that the Spirit of God was *"poured out on all flesh"* at Pentecost—old and young, men and women, everyone ... everywhere.

Or, to put it another way: *"The Holy Land is everywhere."*

Black Elk knew what Jesus knew: the secret of wisdom was to become like little children, as he said:

> "Grown men can learn from very little children, for the hearts of the little children are pure. Therefore, the Great Spirit may show to them many things which older people miss."[6]

He also knew that everyone is connected to the Spirit of God, even if they're unaware of it:

> "Peace will come to the hearts of men when they realize their oneness with the universe. It is everywhere."

This quote reminds me of when Jesus told us that whatever we do to others, we do it to him. Loving God and loving others are the very same thing. The Kingdom of God is within each of us. We don't need to go out and find it, or search for it. The doorway is within us.

I also remember how Jesus stressed his oneness with the Father, and our oneness with him, and the Father, too:

> "On that day you will realize that I am in my Father, and you are in me, and I am in you." (John 14:20)

---

6   Ibid.

Black Elk seems to have been on the same wavelength when he said:

"The first peace, which is the most important, is that which comes within the souls of people when they realize their relationship, their oneness with the universe and all its powers, and when they realize at the center of the universe dwells the Great Spirit, and that its center is really everywhere, it is within each of us."[7]

I also love the way Black Elk describes the reality of the spirit world and this one:

"Crazy Horse dreamed and went into the world where there is nothing but the spirits of all things. That is the real world that is behind this one, and everything we see here is something like a shadow from that one. I knew that the real was yonder and that the darkened dream of it was here." [8]

I've also been very inspired by the writings of Rumi who was a 13th century Persian poet and Sufi mystic who wrote beautiful sayings like these:

"Your task is not to seek for love, but merely to seek and find all the barriers within yourself that you have built against it."

"What you seek is seeking you."

"Yesterday I was clever, so I wanted to change the world. Today, I am wise, so I am changing myself."

"Your wound is the place where the Light enters you."

"Lovers don't finally meet somewhere. They are in each other all along."

---

7 Ibid.

8 Ibid.

"Christian, Jew, Muslim, shaman, Zoroastrian, stone, ground, mountain, river, each has a secret way of being with the mystery, unique and not to be judged."

"Goodbyes are only for those who love with their eyes. For those who love with their heart and soul, there is no such thing as separation."

"Stop acting so small. You are the universe in ecstatic motion."

"Everything in the universe is within you. Ask all from yourself."

"Let the beauty we love be what we do. There are hundreds of ways to kneel and kiss the ground."

"Silence is the language of God. All else is poor translation."

"I searched for God and found only myself. I searched for myself and found only God."

We also find fascinatingly similar sayings to the ones we hear in Christ spoken of in ancient Egyptian proverbs like these:

"The Kingdom of Heaven is within you: and whosoever shall know himself shall find it."

"Know the world in yourself. Never look for yourself in the world, for this would be to project your illusion."

"The key to all problems is the problem of consciousness."

"Man, know thyself and thou shalt know the gods."

One could probably find a few other interesting proverbs from a variety of non-Biblical sources that also convey wisdom and even insight about the Kingdom of God, human nature, and a lot more. For example, in the apocryphal Gospel of Philip we find wisdom like this:

"The Truth is one, and many, for our sakes, to teach us about the One, in love, through the many."

"Farming in this world depends on 4 things: water, earth, air, and light. God's farming also depends on 4 things: faith, hope, love and knowledge. Faith is the earth in which we take root. Hope is the water with which we are nourished. Love is the air through which we grow. Knowledge is the light in which we ripen."

"Love never says it owns something, though it owns everything. Love does not say 'this is mine' or 'that is mine' but rather 'all that is mine is yours.'"

And the Gospel of Thomas contains numerous wisdom sayings like:

"The Kingdom of God is inside you, and all around you. Not in buildings of wood and stone. Split a piece of wood and I am there. Turn a stone and you will find me."

We could literally go on and on. From Socrates to Alan Watts and Eckhart Tolle to Desmond Tutu, there is an endless outpouring of God's wisdom and inspired truth from every tongue and tribe and nation across the globe. Whether a book, or a song, or a film, or even a conversation with a dear friend over coffee, the inspiration of God can surprise us and overwhelm us when we least expect it.

I've heard God's whisper to my heart when I watch a film where a grieving mother cries out to God for answers regarding the death of her son in *Tree Of Life* as scenes of the Universe being created fill the silent void. I've wept as the young man in the film *Into The Wild* realizes, too late, that "happiness is only real when shared," as he dies alone in the wilderness, and I've marveled at the wonder of God's love as expressed in the poetry of Rumi, or the paintings of Jackson Pollock.

God's voice is everywhere. Signs of God's presence, and truth are hidden in plain sight for those who have eyes to see and ears to hear.

So, what writings do you find inspiring? Which voices resonate with your spirit and draw you closer to God? What are the words, poems, songs, lyrics, stories, films, or plays that whisper Truth to your innermost being? Who are the people who inspire you, bless you, heal you, set you free, touch you, affirm you, release you, cleanse you, or teach you like no other?

Jesus promised us there was more to know than we know. The Gospel writers affirmed that more was spoken than we have ever written down.

We should never stop searching. Never stop seeking. Never reach the end of our curiosity about God, Life, Truth, Wisdom, or Love.

We must try to fully embrace this endlessly unfolding Mystery of Christ. It is the river of living water that Jesus promised would flow from within us. This is the abundant life that he said he came to show us. This is what it means to abide in Christ, as Christ abides in you. Not a "knowing" of facts, but a "knowing" that evokes a deep intimacy that transcends knowledge, or vocabulary.

Never settle for a glass of certainty when you can become immersed in the endlessly unfolding ocean of mystery that is Christ.

All the God-breathed writings, and sayings, are to be received as the gifts of God to us. The Spirit of Christ is not limited to the Bible. The Canon is not closed. It will never be closed, but God's Spirit is always at work, always revealing, always enlightening, always breathing truth into us and the entire universe as it has for all eternity.

THE GREAT I AM
IS AN "US"

Why can't I stop thinking about God?
Maybe because God can't stop thinking about me?

*"My thoughts of you are more numerous than the grains of sand on the
beaches of earth."* [Ps. 139:17]

Why can't I stop singing songs about God?
Maybe because God can't stop singing songs of rejoicing over us?

"I am with you,
I am mighty to save,
I rejoice over you
with singing." (Zeph. 3:17)

Did you know God has a favorite song?
That there is a song in heaven the angels cannot stop singing?

It goes like this:

"Peace on earth!
Goodwill to all people!
A child is born,
A son is given,

His name is Love,
God with us!
And the Kingdom of Love
Shall have no end.
Let Love reign!
Let Love rule!
Let Love and Peace come to you."

The Great "I AM" is a
"We" and an "Us"

God is "We"
God is "Us"

God's pronouns are
"We" and "Us"

If God is "We"
And if God is "Us"
How can God be far away?

How can I fail to see God's face
Or hear God's voice?

How can I ever be separated from God
If God is always "We" and "Us"?

Chapter 4

KNOWING LESS
IS MORE

"The truth about forever is that it is happening right now."
SARAH DESSEN

"If you understand it, it's not God."
ST. AUGUSTINE

By now I think you're probably starting to see the point I'm trying to make in this book. But, if not, let me clarify where I'm going with all of this: *Certainty about God is impossible.* Anything we think we know about God must be held loosely because, by definition, God is a Being too wonderful, too magnificent, too astounding for any of us to fully comprehend. At best, we can say, "I think," or "I believe," but none of us can ever say we *know* very much about God. All of our theology falls short. Every doctrine is incomplete. We may have a handful of ideas about God that make sense to us, based on our experience, or a few safe assumptions about God that seem logical. But we all must admit that we could be wrong about at least *some* of what we believe, if not all of it.

What we're left with is faith. Not certainty. What we have to play with are questions. Not answers. What we're talking about is a journey. Not a destination. But, this should give us joy, not fill us with dread.

Yes, the Mystery of God compels us to ask, and seek and knock. Yes, we cannot help but press deeper into the great unknown of God. Yes, we know we will never fully grasp the infinite glory of God in this life. But, that doesn't mean we don't make any progress. Far from it. The path may be endless, but with every passing day, the more we search, the more we question, the more we desire to know and be known by this beautiful, ineffable, exquisite God who has formed us and fashioned us as a reflection of Godself, the one thing we can do is simply this: to draw nearer to the heart of God today than we were yesterday.

Will we ever arrive at our destination? Who can say? But, God is not far away. God is alive within; living and breathing along with us in every moment. How do we know this? We can stop, be still, listen, and experience God's presence anytime we need to. We can trust, by faith, that God will never leave us or forsake us. We can believe that Jesus is in the Father, and the Father is in us, and we are in Christ.

Can we prove any of this scientifically? No. Of course not. But, this is only because the kind of "knowing" we're talking about is closer to love, and joy, and peace; things that cannot be measured, or counted, or weighed or graphed. We may not be able to prove our hearts are filled with love. But, we can certainly know love for ourselves without requiring scientific data to qualify or quantify it for us.

For example, there are things I know that I cannot explain. Some might call these miracles, or signs. And I know that not everyone has experiences like these, but that makes them even more mysterious, and precious to me.

The Invisible Wall

The first time I went to prison, I was nearly shot by a sniper in the guard tower who thought I was trying to escape. How I got there and what led to this potentially deadly experience is an interesting story.

When I was in my mid-twenties, singing and performing in a band had become part of my regular routine. In addition to attending college at the University of Texas at El Paso, and working in the mail room at the Baptist Book Store in town, I was also the lead singer for "Arrival."

After playing together for over 5 years, we had slowly become a very big fish in a pretty small pond, as far as the local band scene went. During our time together we played bars, clubs, youth centers, public schools, College campuses, and even a movie theater, trying to preach the Gospel [as we understood it at the time] to save as many young people as we could with our original alternative rock music.

Eventually, we got connected to the chaplain at a nearby Federal prison, just over the border in New Mexico. La Tuna was a minimum security prison, but you wouldn't know it from the inside. To get accepted to play for the main prisoners within the prison itself, we had to sort of prove ourselves by playing a show for those in the Honor Camp which was just outside the main gate. The Honor Camp was where prisoners who had proven themselves could live in a nicer facility and a smaller community. They were allowed to be outside more often, and presumably had better food options as well as a better shot at scoring an early release or probation based on their good behavior.

When our drummer and I first arrived, we got turned around and missed the dirt road that led to the Honor Camp. We didn't realize we had gone the wrong way until we pulled all the way up to the actual prison itself and then we had to do an awkward U-turn to head back the right way. Once we pulled up, the Chaplain met us in person, shook our hands, and showed us where we would be set up in the center of the outdoor plaza where the prisoners in the Honor Camp lived. After a few minutes, he excused himself. "I need to head back to my office really quick," he said. We assured him we would be fine and he left us there to unload our equipment.

We unloaded our gear first, and then while the drummer set up his kit, I decided to walk around a bit. My concern was for my other bandmates who were running late. I knew they would most likely miss the turn like we did. So, I decided to walk out to the fork in the road to wave them over in the right direction. As I walked, I was also thinking about our upcoming show. There were always things that could go wrong. Broken strings. Forgotten lyrics. The usual stuff. But, I really wanted our concert to go well, so I was praying about that as I walked along the dirt road out towards the intersection. Suddenly it felt like I had walked into a solid brick wall. I stopped dead in my tracks. It was as if a large hand was holding me in place. I had an overwhelming urge to stand perfectly still, as if God were saying, "stop"; although I heard nothing.

After a minute or so I kind of felt stupid. What was I doing standing here in the middle of the road? I even asked God, "Okay, God, why am I standing here?" I heard nothing. But, the urge to stand perfectly still remained.

So, feeling a bit foolish, I just continued to stand there and pray until I saw a truck coming towards me from the main prison. As it got a bit closer I recognized the Chaplain behind the wheel and I raised my hand to wave.

When the truck got closer he screeched to a halt and opened the door to talk to me over the idling engine. "What do you think you're doing?" He sounded a little upset, so I explained my plan to walk out to the cross roads to wave the rest of my band mates the right way.

He just shook his head and glared at me. "Do you see that guard tower behind me?" I looked up and saw a very large guard toward at the nearest corner of the prison yard about 250 yards away.

"Yeah," I said.

"Well, there's a sniper in that tower who just came over the radio asking if he had permission to take a head shot. On you."

What? "Why would he do that?" I asked.

"Because the bed check came up missing one prisoner and the whole facility is on alert. When the sniper saw someone walking away from the prison and out towards the main road, he assumed you were probably the escaped prisoner they were looking for."

Before I could explain, he just shook his head in disgust. "Never mind. Just slowly raise your hands in the air and walk carefully towards the truck," he said.

As I did, he ducked by inside the cab and spoke into the radio: "All clear. It's just one of the kids playing a concert tonight at the Honor Camp."

That was probably the most intense spiritual experience of my life. At least, it's the only one that had to do with life and death. But, it wasn't the only one.

Special Delivery

A few years later, after I had gotten married, graduated college and moved to Southern California—in that order—my wife Wendy and I ended up joining a Vineyard church in Newport Beach.

This was our first real experience with more Charismatic believers, and, for the most part, it was very positive.

One evening I was attending our small group gathering at a friend's house. Wendy was at home watching our boys that night, as we took turns, so it was my time to be there.

Just before the worship and teaching was over, I noticed a man walk in the front door and stand at the back of the room while our host was wrapping up his lesson. I had never seen this guy in any of our other gatherings before, but I did notice he was wearing a UPS uniform, complete with the little brown shorts and the short-sleeved brown shirt with the logo on the chest.

As we were getting ready to dismiss and head into the kitchen for snacks and refreshments, the UPS driver raised his hand as if he wanted to say something.

"Yeah, Steve?" the host said. "You have something to add?"

Steve, the UPS driver, cleared his throat and spoke up: "I was just wondering if anyone here was feeling spiritually dry and needed some prayer, I feel like God might want me to pray for them," he said.

Our host didn't blink an eye. "Is there anyone here tonight who feels the way Steve described?"

No one raised their hand, except for my friend, Greg, who was sitting right next to me. After a few awkward seconds passed, I also raised my hand. No one else took the bait.

So, after a quick prayer to bless our refreshments, everyone stood up and went into the kitchen to fill up their plates and small talk.

Everyone except for me, and Greg, and the UPS man, Steve.

Once the three of us were alone in the living room, Steve asked my friend, Greg, if he could lay his hands on his shoulder and pray for him. Greg said, "Sure," and Steve began to pray.

This is where I started to roll my eyes. Because Steve was praying some very specific things about Greg that I knew there was no way he could know. Neither of us had ever met this guy before, so I could tell this was going to be a complete waste of our time. My only hope was that it would be over soon and I could still grab a piece of that pecan pie I had seen in the kitchen before it was all gone.

After Steve finished praying for Greg, he moved over to me, laid his hands on my shoulder, and began to pray. I braced myself for the nonsense.

But, instead of nonsense, I was startled to hear Steve mention specific things about my life he couldn't have known. Things about my family, my finances, my background. I was starting to realize something very strange was taking place. But, then it got much stranger.

Near the end of the prayer, Steve paused. He waited a few seconds, and then he seemed to hear something. He nodded silently and then he said something that nearly knocked me to the floor.

As he was praying over me, he mentioned a very specific question that I had asked God as I was driving, alone, in my car on the way home from work the day before. It wasn't a typical question. It wasn't general. It was very, very specific. Steve reminded me of my question, and then, to my complete surprise, he told me God's answer to the question.

I melted on the spot. Hot tears were rolling down my face. My heart was quivering. My mind was reeling. "How could he know this?" I wondered. Only God and I knew what I had asked. I hadn't even said those words out loud, much less shared them with anyone else. This could only mean one thing: God was speaking to Steve and delivering the answer to my question, via UPS.

Talk about next day delivery! I was stunned, blessed, touched and overwhelmed.

When Steve finished his prayer I looked up and wiped away my tears. I glanced over at Greg, who was also drying his eyes. I couldn't help but ask him, "Was any of that stuff he prayed over you accurate?" Greg nodded. "Every single word."

I nodded back. "Me too, dude. What was that?"

We both laughed and cried and shared how what Steve had prayed over us had been exactly what we needed to hear in that moment.

Unexpected Gift

Several years later, Wendy and I had moved to another house and helped to start a new Vineyard church in Tustin, California with a few of our friends. I had begun the habit of praying for our family, our church, and the people we were serving in our community, whenever I woke up in the middle of the night. Which, strangely, seemed to always happen around 3:30 in the morning for some reason.

On this particular night, I woke up in the bed, stood up quietly and made my way to our living to pray.

As usual, I sat down on our sofa and began to pray for our family, our church, the people we were serving in our community and a few other things that were on my mind that evening.

After a few minutes or so, I finished praying and stood up to go back to bed, but about halfway across the floor I stopped and realized I wasn't really that sleepy. So, I decided to turn around and go back to the sofa to pray a bit more.

As I sat down again and started to pray again, I began to notice something strange. My words weren't making any sense. It sounded like gibberish. But, in my mind I knew who and what I was praying about.

It was very odd. One part of my brain was saying to the other part, "Hey, those words don't make sense," and then the other part would say, "Yeah, I know. Why is this happening?"

I didn't feel anything spiritual or tingly at all. It was the most normal, average moment imaginable. Except for the fact that my words were coming out strange.

Another weird thing I noticed was that, when I changed the focus of my prayers, the cadence and pattern of my words changed, too. Praying for my kids was entirely different than when I prayed for my parents, or when I prayed for my friends. It was as if each group of people had a unique language or inflection to go along with it.

The other strange thing was that I couldn't stop it. It was like a fire hose. I could aim it at this prayer need, or that concern, but I couldn't shut it off. It was like a river of unintelligible words gushing out of my mouth like water from a fire hydrant.

But it gets weirder than that. Just as I was starting to pay attention to certain words and phrases that I was saying with my mouth, my brain had the thought: "I wish I knew what these words meant … " but before I could even finish that sentence it was as if an inner switch was thrown and suddenly I understood the words: This one meant "protection," and this one meant "strength" and that other one meant "peace", and as each word was uttered on my tongue I knew what it was in the same instant.

Eventually, the torrential flow of glossolalia began to slow down and about that time, Wendy carefully walked over to me.

Apparently I had woken her up with my exuberant prayers. She sat down next to me on the couch and put her hand on my knee. "Are you okay?"

I looked up at her. My own words had returned. "Yeah, I think so," I said. I could tell she wasn't so sure.

"I think I just spoke in tongues."

She nodded. "That's what it sounded like."

The next day when I went into the Church office where I worked, I told everyone about what had happened. They were overjoyed, to say the least.

To some of them I'm sure it was a sign that I was filled with the Holy Spirit or something. But, to me, I had always been filled with the Spirit. It was just that my main gifting was expressed in teaching or service or compassion.

Our Church secretary was my friend, Barb. She was especially excited to hear about what I had experienced. But, honestly, I just assumed that it was a one-time thing. So, a few weeks later when she asked me if I was enjoying praying in tongues now, I was taken aback.

"No, it hasn't happened to me since that night," I said. Barb laughed. "You can do it anytime you want to," she said. "Have you tried to pray in tongues again since that night?"

It had honestly never even occurred to me. "No," I said.

Barb shook her head and tried not to laugh. "God gave you the gift of tongues," she said. "Next time you're praying just try to say some of those words again and see what happens."

Guess what? She was right. I really did have the gift of tongues, and I really could pray that same way anytime I wanted.

What I find so astounding about this experience is that I had never once asked God to give me the gift of tongues. In fact, as a good Southern Baptist boy, I would have never asked for that gift in a million years, and God knew that.

So, I think that's why God gave it to me out of the blue. Because God knew it would bless me more than I did, and it turns out God—as always—was right.

Nothing But Net

My oldest son, Dylan, was around 17 years old when our little house church family was going strong at our new house in Orange, California a few years after my spontaneous tongues experience.

Dylan had made a comment about how he had never heard God's voice or had any spiritual experiences with God. Several people asked him if he would be okay if they prayed over him about that. He said, "Okay, sure."

So, a few of us gathered around him as he sat on our sofa and placed our hands on him to pray for him. It was all pretty standard stuff. Dylan just sat there, quietly. People prayed and asked God to reveal Godself to him.

Eventually, everyone had prayed except for me and so I placed my hand over Dylan's heart to offer a prayer of my own.

As I did so, I clearly saw in my mind's eye something very unusual. It was a very large basketball and it was on fire. Like, it was a giant ball of fire and yet it had those same markings that basketballs have.

I had no clue what that could possibly mean. In fact, it was so strange and so unspiritual that I almost didn't even mention it as I started to pray for him but it just did not go away. All I could see was that stupid flaming basketball over his heart.

So, against my better judgement, I said it out loud: "Dylan, I don't know what this means exactly, but as soon as I put my hand over your heart I started to see this giant flaming basketball. It's still there. I think, maybe, it means that God has put a fire in your heart and it's like a giant ball of fire." I mumbled a few other things, and then we all said, "Amen" and slowly stood up and backed away to see if Dylan had anything to say.

Someone asked him, "Dylan, did you feel anything or did God speak to you at all?" Dylan's expression remained as it was. He wasn't crying. He wasn't smiling. He was just sort of casually sitting there as we looked at him. Then he said this: "The only thing I saw, as soon as you guys started praying over me was this giant flaming basketball."

I couldn't believe it. Then he said, "When Dad said he saw that same fireball I thought that was weird. But, I saw it, too."

That's when I started to cry. Because God had given us both such a unique and strange image at the same time. No one in our family was really into sports. There was no possible way it could be anything other than God speaking to Dylan's heart using that image of a flaming basketball.

It was like a spiritual alley-oop from Jesus to me, and then to Dylan for the windmill slam-dunk.

Mysterious Ways

When I was just out of High School, my family moved out of the mobile home we had lived in for almost 8 years and into a house a few miles away.

As we were moving the very last of our things out of the trailer and into the back of my Dad's pickup truck, he fell off a ladder and hit his head on the concrete.

It was a complete head-first dive into the ground from around six feet off the ground.

By the time I got over to him he was standing up and acting as if everything was okay.

"Are you sure?" my Mom and I kept asking him.

"I'm fine," he said. "Just clumsy, I guess."

So, here's the weird part. We were all in different cars. My Mom had her car. I was driving mine, and my Dad was driving his truck.

We all took off in our own vehicles and drove towards our new house. My Dad, as usual, gunned the engine and pulled ahead of both of us, losing us at the first stop light.

That's when I started to get worried. What if he hit his head so hard he forgets how to get to our new house? How would we ever find him if he gets turned around?

Regretting the decision to allow him to drive a moving vehicle so soon after hitting his head like that, I started driving faster to see if I could catch up to him.

When I finally pulled up to our house my Dad's truck was parked in our driveway, but he was half out of the car with one leg on the ground and the other still inside his truck. I parked quickly and ran over to him.

"Are you okay, Dad?"

He had a confused look on his face. "This is not our house," he said.

"Yes, it is, Dad. You just bought it, remember?"

He looked at me like he wasn't even sure who I was. Eventually we got him inside the house but then his behavior became more erratic. He started crying for no reason. He couldn't remember the name of his best friend. He kept asking if he could take a shower. We told him we needed him to go to the Emergency Room. Eventually, he agreed and managed to get him into the car. My Mom drove this time.

After a few X-Rays they gave us the bad news. "Mr. Giles has four damaged vertebrae in his neck," the Doctor explained. "One is cracked, one is crushed, and these two at the top are powdered. It's a miracle he isn't paralyzed."

So, my Dad was given a neck brace and scheduled for a CAT Scan a few days later to determine the extent of his injuries.

A few hours before his CAT Scan, our Baptist pastor and one of our Deacons dropped by my Dad's room to pray for him.

Please keep in mind that when a Southern Baptist prays for a miraculous healing it usually goes something like this: *"Dear Lord, we pray that you would heal brother Giles here—but we know you probably won't—so, give him peace and comfort him in his afflictions. Amen!"*

So, we weren't very optimistic, to say the least. In fact, the Doctor had already told my Dad that if the best spinal surgeon in the world operated on his neck, there would be a 50/50 chance of his being paralyzed for life. "But, we don't have the best spinal surgeon in the world," he said. "So, your chances go down from there."

That's why, when the Doctor gave us the results of the CAT Scan by starting off with, "Mr. Giles, I am so sorry," we all believed the worst. But, then he continued: "I'm holding your X-Ray in this hand showing your vertebrae are crushed, cracked and powdered, but in my other hand I'm looking at the CAT Scan and you're neck is completely fine. I don't know what happened."

My Dad sat up in the bed and shouted, "I know what happened. Jesus healed me!"

That was a long time ago. My Dad lived another thirty or so years after that without any neck pain or headaches. He really had been miraculously healed.

I love telling that story, but I can't tell it now without adding the fact that my Dad is no longer with us. He passed away suddenly due to complications from Pneumonia a few weeks after his 77th birthday in August of 2020.

That's an interesting story as well.

Passing Away

My Dad smoked cigarettes since he was around 12 years old. I've seen pictures of him as a kid holding a cigarette in one hand and a BB gun in the other.

So, it's no surprise that my Dad ended up with COPD and needing oxygen to breathe for the last 20 years of his life. That breathing issue is why we had to send him to the hospital when he contracted pneumonia.

While in the hospital, his dementia added to the challenges of treating him. The doctors and nurses couldn't get him to cooperate with them. He refused to allow them to use the machines that were designed to loosen up the phlegm in his lungs so he could breathe.

All of this took place just as COVID-19 was ramping up in August of 2020. That meant the hospitals were overcrowded. It also meant no one in the family could come visit him while he was there. Eventually, they just sent him home to recover as there was nothing more they could do for him.

Two days later he died. But, during those two days he was at home, I got to wash my Dad's feet, shave him, and hold him. I got tell him how much I loved him, and he made a point, the night before he passed away, of taking me by the hand and looking me in the eye and saying, "I am so proud of you, son; of your books, your writing, the father and husband you are … I love you," he said.

"I love you, too, Dad."

The next morning, at around 6:32 a.m., my Mom came into the room he was resting in to find him unconscious. She called 911 and tried to revive him, but he was gone.

One thing strange about the way she found him was that he was wearing his glasses. He had also apparently taken a sip of water from the glass beside his bed because it had moved from where it was the night before.

It was as if my Dad had awakened from sleep, sat up in bed, taken a sip of water, put on his glasses, and taken off his oxygen line—which he never took off around the house—and then fell back on to the bed, and into the arms of Jesus.

Do I know this is what happened? Not exactly. Of course, it could have been different. No one was there. We don't really know. But, we *can* extrapolate based on a few of the facts. My Dad wasn't in distress when my Mom found him. He didn't look as if he had been gasping for breath. He didn't knock anything over. He very intentionally had taken off his oxygen line and put on his glasses—as if to get a better look at something he was seeing—and then he fell backwards on to the bed, which is the way my Mom found him.

The point is, whatever the sequence of events, my Dad closed his eyes in this world and opened them again in the next.

He lives and breathes now in a place beyond our imagination. My Dad is immersed in the reality of the Great Mystery in a way you and I can only dream of.

Wherever my Dad is now, I will be there soon. So will you. In fact, maybe, in some very strange way, we already are.

Greater Mystery

The great philosopher Aristotle once said, "Time is the most unknown of all unknown things." That was nearly 2,500 years ago, but it's still as true today as it was then. Some of the smartest people on the planet can't really explain what Time is, or how it works. What we believe about Time is that it's a dimension, and that it's also a measurement. In other words, it can help us understand when something happens, or happened, and that it can tell us how long something lasted, or how long ago it took place.

Space, like Time, is also a Dimension. Yet, we can move through Space at will, in any direction, but we can only move through Time in one direction: Forward. As far as we know, it is not possible for us to leap forward into the future, or to skip back to the past. But, according to Albert Einstein, "Time and Space are modes by which we think, and not conditions in which we live." That means even though we all experience Time as a linear process where one moment is followed by the next, and the next, that's not exactly how Time itself operates.

What Einstein suggests is that Time may not exist as a fundamental property of the Universe, but as an emergent property. What's the difference? Well, emergent properties don't exist in any individual components of a system, but they do exist for the system as a whole. For example, individual water molecules aren't wet, and they don't react to the tides, but the entire ocean does feel wet, and it is expressed in the motion of the tides. Another example would be the way a film, which is merely a series of still images, can appear to have a fluid motion when viewed in sequence at a very rapid pace. The film seems to reflect motion and the passage of time, but that is an illusion.

In reality, each individual frame of the film is completely motionless and never changes. So, the passage of time and motion we experience when we watch a film are emergent properties of the way we perceive those still images when projected against a screen and viewed at 24 frames per second.

So, the question Einstein poses is this: Could the physics of Time somehow be a similar illusion? Could it be that what we see, and even experience, as the passage of Time moving forward from past to present to future, is actually not reality?

Well, the short answer is: There's no reason for us to assume that Time only flows in one direction. Our perception of Time is linear, but Time itself is not. Time, like Space, just is. We experience the dimension of Space as we move through it. We never experience the totality of all Space at once, but only the area of whatever space we happen to occupy at that moment. The same is true of time. Time extends in every direction at once, but we only experience whatever area of time we happen to be in at the present moment.

Space and Time are both three-dimensional. That means anyone's perception of either is relative to their experience, but their individual experience of either is not the totality of it.

The way we experience Time is part of the problem. Because we experience Time in a linear fashion, we tend to believe that all that exists is this present moment. The past is erased and the future is a void yet to be filled. To us, the answer is assumed to be whatever we experience in the ever-flowing eyeblink between past and future that we call "the Present", or "Now." But recent developments in Quantum Physics suggest that the future and the past both exist eternally while the present moment is—for lack of a better term—an illusion.

Isaac Newton, the father of classical "Newtonian" physics, taught us that it was possible to measure and even predict the position and velocity of every particle in the universe, leading to a deterministic view of reality. He believed that it was possible to prove that everyone was experiencing the same, absolute, clearly-definable moment called "Now." But, today's physicists now know that Newton was totally wrong. Newton assumed that all particles, all observers, and all points in space were ruled by a single, constantly-ticking universal clock. If true, this would mean that it was possible to define a notion of "now" that everyone would agree on.

However, with the rise of Quantum Physics, scientists now know that there is no one single universal clock, and that it is more difficult—and in some cases impossible—accurately predict the position and velocity of a every particle in the universe. Especially once you begin to look at electrons, protons, photons, molecules and other quantum particles. In fact, what scientists realize now is that one can either predict the position of a particle, but not the velocity, or one can measure the velocity of a particle, but not the position of that same particle in space. This means that Newton was wrong. We cannot accurately predict these two things—position and velocity—at all.

Further studies also found that Time itself doesn't only follow one predetermined path, but that Time exists all at once across all possible dimensions of Space. So, Time doesn't have a particular direction, and there's no preferred "present" reality. Time is just a dimension, like Space, and we only observe the flow of time in one direction—similar to the way a film works when we play those individual still images at 24 frames per second to create the illusion of motion and the passage of time.

Having said all of that—and I hope you were able to keep up with most of it—the point I wanted to make is simply this: Time isn't linear. The Past, the Present, and the Future already exist in one single block. Scientists even refer to this as the "Block Universe" theory for this very reason.

So, if Time isn't linear, and if someone could step outside of Space and Time and observe it from that perspective, they could see everything all at once. They could zoom in and find me sitting here typing this sentence as I sit at my laptop in my home office, and then they could turn things slightly to view another facet of my life and see me playing with my friends in the schoolyard when I was in Third Grade, and then turn it once more to see me getting married to

Wendy when I was in my Twenties, and then turn it again to see how I died. All of it is already there. My experience of my life isn't like that, but Time is like that.

Another way to illustrate how our experience of Time differs from the reality of Time, is to think of our present reality as the music encoded into the grooves of a vinyl record. We experience the present moment like the needle that travels around the spinning record, but the entire song exists all at once on the record. You could stop the turntable with your hand, roll it backwards, or forwards, or even lift the record off and look at it as a single object. So, in other words, no one is "playing" the music of our present reality. It just is.[9]

This is why I can say—as I did just a few pages back—that wherever my Dad went after he passed from this reality and entered the Great Mystery beyond, I'm probably there with him, and you are too, and so is everyone who has ever, or will ever, live. Because at the moment we leave this Block Universe reality, we step outside of Space and Time and we enter a reality apart from this one. In that great beyond, everything is "now." So, when I close my eyes and breathe my last breath in this body, and open my eyes in the next reality after this one, I will turn and see my Father open his eyes for the first time, too. We'll both look at each other and say, "Hey there! You made it!" because we will both arrive in that place at the same moment. So will you and everyone else.

If all of this discussion of Time and Space is making your head hurt, or if you think it's all just speculative nonsense, let me remind you that, whenever astronomers look into deep space with their telescopes, they

---

9   Much of what I say in this section of the chapter comes from the episode, "Do The Present and Future Exist?" on the *PBS Space Time* YouTube channel: https://www.youtube.com/watch?v=EagNUvNfsUI

are, in fact, looking into the distant past. How so? Well, when we look at a galaxy 140 million light years away, this means the light emitted by that galaxy travelled 140 million years before reaching us on earth. Therefore, we're not looking at this galaxy as it today. We're looking at that galaxy as it was 140 million years ago. This means that the stars you see when you look up at the night sky have probably been dead for several million years, and their light won't flicker out for another million years after all of us are dead and gone.

So, a telescope is a sort of time machine that allows us to look at what the universe was like a few hundred million years ago. We're actually not sure what the larger universe looks like right now, because by the time the light travels across the vast distance of space, it won't be "now" anymore. It will be the past. Even within our own solar system, whenever you look at a planet like Neptune, for example, the light you're seeing took 4 hours to reach us. So, we're only seeing what Neptune was like 4 hours ago, not what it looks like right now.

More Time

One of the more beautiful things about the universe is that it is endlessly unfolding itself. Maybe we are too?

I mean, if Time isn't linear, then maybe we need to rethink reality and how we as human beings exist within this dimension.

Under the previous assumptions about time, I tended to see myself as the person who exists in this very moment; this constant "now" of the present. But, that's not entirely true, is it? I mean, I am alive in 1966 at my birth, and that's me in 1975 playing the saxophone, and that's me in 1985 graduating from High School, and that's also me getting married in 1989, and also me moving to California in 1993, and also me moving to Idaho in 2018, and then again moving to

El Paso in 2019, and it's also me waking up three days ago to drive someone to the airport. All of those are me. The baby, the toddler, the teenager, the young adult, the college student, the older, wiser author sitting here now, and the [hopefully] much older version of me that will one day breathe his very last breath; all of these are the same me. They are all—at the very same time—who I am as a person.

Another way of saying this is that, if you asked me to hand you an apple, I would not take a sharp knife and cut off a paper-thin slice to give you. That would be stupid, and weird. But, in the same way, if you asked me to show you who Keith Giles is, and I were to show you a photo of myself here and now, that would be like handing you that slice of apple instead of the whole thing. Because, as with that apple, a snapshot of myself in one single moment of time is an incomplete expression of what my physical existence really is within all of Space and Time.

Now, if this is true, then who am I? How do I imagine myself as one continuous person across every moment of time and space in which I have existed, and continue to exist? Am I more like an elongated Play-Dough snake stretching across the years from my birth to my death? Am I like a series of still photographs placed one after the other that run forward at 24 frames per second in some cosmic movie theater? Am I like a song being played on a long, continuous groove etched into the surface of a mystical vinyl record in God's record collection?

The truth is, it's all sort of a mystery, isn't it? The universe is unfolding. Deep calls to deep. All things are being made new. What we are is a mystery. What we will be is unknown. After we die, where will go? What will happen next?

None of us really knows.

But that's okay, isn't it? I mean, how boring would it be if we knew how the story ended, or how it was all going to work out? No one likes a predictable plot. We want to be surprised, amazed, maybe even shocked to discover how deep, and wide, and long the rabbit hole goes.

If anything, it should give us comfort to know that we don't have all the answers. It's okay to ask questions. It's even okay to have doubts.

The original ending of the earliest Gospel—the Gospel of Mark—ends with this startling admission:

> "So, they went out and fled from the tomb, for terror and amazement had seized them; and they said nothing to anyone, for they were afraid." (Mark 16:8)

What a way to end a Gospel, right? The disciples of Jesus find his empty tomb. A "young man dressed in a white robe" [v.5] tells them that Jesus is alive, but they never see or encounter the risen Jesus. That's in the newer, longer ending of Mark, and in the other Gospel accounts, but not in Mark's Gospel. Here, they find an empty tomb, hear from a young man sitting nearby that Jesus is alive again, and then their reaction is to flee from the tomb in terror and we're left with this faith-building nugget: "and they said nothing to anyone, for they were afraid." Wow. That's a bit of a downer, isn't it? But the added ending isn't that much better because twice it makes the point that many who heard that Jesus was alive "would not believe it" (v.11), and "did not believe them." (v.13)

What this tells us is that, to those earliest Christians, doubt wasn't a sin, confusion wasn't uncommon and that amazement was par for the course.

We could use a little bit of that refreshing honesty today, I believe. Admitting that we're scared, or that we don't always believe, or that we doubt something about our faith shouldn't be a sign of falling away from Christ. It should be seen as evidence that we're walking in the same path as those first disciples; Unsure. Uncertain. Doubtful. Yet full of amazement and wonder at the same time.

When Thomas doubted the resurrection, Jesus didn't mock him for wanting answers. He was blessed because he believed what he saw with his own eyes. His questions were valid. His doubts were reasonable. His skepticism was taken seriously.

Yes, Jesus did use this encounter as an opportunity to remind us that those who believe without requiring hard proof were blessed even more than those who believed because they found their answers. Not because God wants us to have blind faith, but because faith itself was never really about seeing, or knowing. It has always been about belief in spite of what you see, or don't see.

This is why I believe we need to embrace the beauty of mystery. Because we follow a Messiah who taught by asking questions instead of giving answers. Because we realize that the God we're after can't be understood by the sharing of information, but only by stepping into the vast ocean of Divine Presence so we can experience for ourselves the God who is "with us", and promises never to leave or forsake us.

Chapter 5

OUR MEANING-MAKING, PATTERN-SEEKING BRAINS

"When you change the way you look at things,
the things you look at change"
MAX PLANCK, NOBEL PHYSICIST

"Everyone wants to understand art. Why not try to understand
the song of a bird? Why does one love the night, flowers,
everything around one without trying to understand them?
But in the case of art, people have to understand."
PABLO PICASSO

In our ongoing quest to speak of all that we *do not know* of God, it might be more useful to challenge all that we believe we already know about everything else. When we do, we might just discover that we know less about those things we think we *do* know.

Our brains are truly wonderful organs. Not only does it control essential heart and lung functions for us automatically, it also receives and processes neural information, sensory data from our eyes, ears, nose and nerve endings, and coordinates movement, thought, and decision-making all at the same time. It also handles sleeping, pain perception, danger-avoidance, intuition, walking, dancing, speaking, regulates body temperature, circadian rhythms, hunger, memory, learning, emotions, hormones, abstract thinking, and pretty much everything else anyone ever needs to thrive.

Another fascinating bit of trivia concerning the way our brain functions is in the way it can be hacked. Yes, we can literally hack our own brains—and sometimes even the brains of other people—due to the plasticity of the human brain. In other words, there are ways to change the ways we think, or feel, or behave if we know how.

One of those ways to hack our brains is to change our body position or posture. For example, whenever you become interested in something, you tend to lean forward and focus your attention on it. This shift in your body is not only an indication of how your brain is reacting, it can actually be used to create that same feeling in your brain by shifting your position. In other words, if you ask someone to show you what an eager learner looks like, they will most likely sit up, lean forward, and focus their eyes on you. In that same motion, their brains will also begin to shift into learning mode. The same is true if you ask someone to show you what a disinterested learner looks like. They will probably slouch in their chair, look at the ceiling, play with their pencil and maybe even utter a deep sigh of boredom for added effect. But, when they shift their body into these actions, their brain waves also shift into disinterested mode. Simply put, when you change your body, you change your brain.

This hacking takes many different forms. Sometimes a hypnotist, or an illusionist can trick your brain using auto-suggestion, slight of hand, mentalism, or a combination of these, to make you act a certain way, or convince you of something that isn't necessarily true, or real. This can be as harmless as a card trick, or as dangerous as cult-leader who convinces you to turn your life over to them.

Another fascinating way our brains can be hacked is in something we call the *Placebo Effect*. This is when someone with some perceived authority—usually a doctor or physician—tells us that we can expect certain outcomes if we follow a prescribed treatment plan and those who follow that plan experience the promised outcomes, even if the treatment contains no active ingredients.

This perplexing phenomenon is, in fact, so common, that drug trials must always demonstrate a better success rate than the placebo in order to become approved for wide consumption.

To put it another way, there is an entire field of scientific research to support the validity of the placebo effect as a proven and documented method of healing the body using only the power of suggestion. Perception seems to be the key factor in the success of the placebo. In other words, people first have to believe that the placebo can heal them. They have to believe that the doctors prescribing the placebo are capable. They have to believe that it's possible for them to experience healing. If all of these factors are aligned, there's a very good chance that the power of suggestion alone is enough to produce the desired results. Therefore, there is a direct correlation in the minds of patients concerning medical treatments and their efficacy. If they believe the drugs will work, they probably will, even if there are no medicinal properties.

It also turns out that there are varying degrees of placebo effectiveness. According to researchers, a placebo capsule works better than a placebo tablet, and a placebo injection is more successful than a capsule, but is not better than a placebo device. It also turns out that a long talk with your trusted physician about your treatment plan increases the effectiveness of the placebo. Taking two placebos is better than one, and taking a more expensive placebo works better than a cheaper one. Also, any placebo that's branded and professionally packaged works better than taking a generic pill with no markings at all.

Color also impacts the effectiveness of placebos. Sleeping aids work better if they're blue. Pain relivers work better if they're red. Yellow placebos make better anti-depressants.

Simply put, the effectiveness of the placebo is directly related to how sophisticated and elaborate the treatment process is. The more we believe we're being given real medicine from a trusted physician, the more likely we are to experience the desired results—even though the entire thing is completely due to tricking our brains into believing what we're told and experiencing exactly what we've been told to experience.

The bottom line is that placebos can actually create very real changes in our bodies, even though there's nothing really going on except the power of belief.

Scientific studies have shown that placebos can cause the brain to release its own natural pain-killing chemicals to soothe the suffering from migraine headaches and even release dopamine to alleviate the symptoms of Parkinson's disease. What's more, placebos can reduce stress, remove anxiety, or even change our moods. Or, maybe we should say, our brains can do those things if we first believe we're being given medicine that is supposed to do those things. It's not the placebo that does anything at all, really. Other than convince our brains that it works so that our brain call trick our body into healing itself.

Believe it or not, the placebo effect has become so prevalent in recent years that more and more new drugs fail to pass the placebo test, and older drugs are starting to perform worse than placebos. For example, drugs like Prozac perform worse today against placebos than when they were first introduced in 1986. Even patients who are told upfront that they are being given a placebo experience positive results. All of this means the placebo effect appears to be growing stronger with every passing generation.[10]

So, the reality is that our brains can do more than most of us even realize. Our expectations, our beliefs, our attitudes, and even our posture can change the way we feel, heal our pain, and sometimes even alter our consciousness.

Doesn't this make you wonder how all of this is possible? Aren't you filled with a sense of mystery about how our brains can be programmed to heal our bodies with as much—if not more—success than most prescription drugs? Even scientists are baffled as to why it happens. They can only confirm that it does happen.

Rewiring Our Brains

One thing I've experienced over the years is how when people undergo spiritual deconstruction they can end up caught in something like a toxic feedback loop of endlessly negative feelings and thoughts surrounding their newfound beliefs. I've noticed it especially in those who deconstruct their views on the way Church should function, but it's also something that people wrestle with as they begin to change their views on Eternal Torment, or Penal Substitution, or the Inerrancy of Scripture.

Here's how it usually works: The person begins to question one of these doctrines of faith. They study to subject and eventually realize that what they were told about this doctrine isn't exactly true. They feel

---

10 From the YouTube series *It's Okay To Be Smart* episode "How The Placebo Effect Tricks Your Brain" https://www.youtube.com/watch?v=JcPwIQ6GCj8

angry, betrayed and manipulated. This initial outrage is quite normal and we shouldn't try to suppress it. But, the problem comes when the person's anger concerning this doctrinal shift continues to dominate their thoughts and permeate their daily life. They simply cannot stop being angry and triggered by this information. It prevents them from moving forward in their spiritual growth and development process.

As an example, I can remember specific people who came into our house church community years ago who could never seem to talk about anything when we came together except how foolish they were for ever believing in the top-down, hierarchical business model of Church they once participated in. First-time visitors or new members were always given plenty of time to vent as they processed their transition from Institutional Church into our more organic, community model of sharing all things equally and practicing what the New Testament calls the "one-another" commands.

However, once someone had been given a few meetings to work all of that toxic outrage out of their system, it was time to let go of that anger and begin actually living out the good fruit of this new way of being church together.

The good news, as we've already seen, is that our brains have a wonderful plasticity and this means we can actually hack our brains and re-learn new ways of thinking that allow us to let go of the endless toxicity and turn the corner into a more positive experience of our newfound beliefs.

One of the best ways to do this is to practice gratitude. Yes, gratitude, it turns out, is an excellent hack for escaping the negative feedback loops generated by our spiritual deconstruction process.

As researchers from the University of California at Davis recently discovered, subjects who kept a daily journal of things they were grateful for experienced dramatically better results than those in the study who either kept a journal of negative experiences, or wrote about whatever they wanted.

According to the 2015 study,

"The gratitude group reported feeling more optimistic and positive about their lives than the other groups. In addition, the gratitude group was more physically active and reported fewer visits to a doctor than those who wrote only about their negative experiences."[11]

Others who have researched the physical effects of gratitude have discovered even more promising results. For example, those who practice gratitude sleep better, have fewer feelings of anxiety and less depression. Gratitude also corresponds to having more energy, reduced inflammation and less risk of heart failure, even for those who have a family history of heart problems.[12]

This type of research has been especially revealing when it comes to how gratitude impacts our brain. One recent neurological experiment at UCLA used magnetic resonance imaging to measure brain activity as participants experienced gratitude. What they found was *increased activity in the anterior cingulate cortex and medial prefrontal cortex— those areas associated with moral and social cognition, empathy, reward and value judgement.*[13] Because of this, researchers have concluded

---

11 "Neuroscience Reveals: Gratitude Literally Rewires Your Brain To Be Happier" from *The Daily Health Post*, Oct. 10, 2020. https://dailyhealthpost.com/gratitude-rewires-brain-happier/?utm_source=link&utm_medium=fb&utm_campaign=sq&utm_content=dhp&fbclid=IwAR0v1og5jCw1DqJUd1sjoRxgw04K6PvP0_NNfEAhaI9A0EfWrkxOpZuwq00

12 "4 Real Risk Factors For Heart Disease You Shouldn't Ignore", *The Daily Health Post* Editorial, Sept. 20, 2018: https://dailyhealthpost.com/4-real-risk-factors-for-heart-disease-you-need-to-know/

13 Ibid.

that gratitude supports a positive attitude towards others and relieves stress in those who practice it.

Gratitude, they found, also activates the hypothalamus in the brain which affects the human metabolism, stress and regulates hormones related to emotional responses, appetite and sleep. And the impact on the brain was transformative as the study continued to show that:

"The positive influence of gratitude on mental health continues past a particular event if the emotion is relived ... subjects who participated in gratitude letter writing showed both behavioral increases in gratitude and significantly greater neural modulation by gratitude in the medial prefrontal cortex three months later."[14]

Further studies showed that gratitude also impacts:

- Reduced thoughts of suicide
- Brain function on a chemical level
- Feelings of self-worth
- Increased compassion for others
- Improved relationships with others

So, if we really hope to rewire our brains and experience the freedom and joy of spiritual reconstruction, gratitude is a very important place to begin. Here's why: Our Deconstruction process is very naturally focused on what's wrong with religion and specifically the theological framework we were born into. This is necessary for Deconstruction. We can't possibly deconstruct our faith and question our theology without this critical questioning and examination of our faith.

But, once we've done this, we need to switch gears mentally and shift from being critical and searching for what's wrong to becoming

---

14   Ibid.

more focused on the good things; we need to start looking for what's right and celebrate whatever is true, whatever is noble, whatever is pure, whatever is lovely, whatever is admirable— and if anything is excellent or praiseworthy, to think about such things. [See Phil. 4:8]

If we can learn to practice gratitude, we can rewire our brains to see the positive and our entire body—our attitude, our heart, our emotions, our capacity to enjoy life, our sense of freedom, and our physical and emotional health—will improve along with our change in perspective.

So, if you'd like to move into this new, uncharted territory of Reconstruction, I'd suggest keeping a daily journal of thanksgiving. Start writing down everything you're thankful for and watch how it changes your life.

Another great thing to start doing is to express gratitude to people and crank up the appreciation factor for those people in your life who bless you. Let them know about it. Look them in the eyes and say, "That really blessed me. Thank you so much!"

While you're at it, don't forget to stop and celebrate your own accomplishments each day. Appreciate yourself. Be grateful for your successes in life. Take note of them. Write them down.

One other great idea is to start keeping an annual "Jar of Remembrance." Our family has been doing this for about 5 years now. Every time something great happens in our life, we write it down on a slip of paper, date it, fold it up and place it into a small glass jar. At the end of the year, we sit down at the table together and celebrate New Year's Eve by taking turns opening up those slips of paper and reading out loud to one another the blessings we've experienced over the last year. When we're all done, we place those slips of paper in an envelope, write the year on it, and seal it up. Then we're ready to start all over again on January 1 with an empty jar just waiting to fill up with blessings again.

A few years ago, our house church family really started to get excited about practicing gratitude and one of our dear sisters in the group decided to take it to an entirely different level. Here's what she decided to do, in her own words:

"In my prayers, the word 'gratitude' has kept coming up and I felt the Lord nudging me to take it more seriously and put it into a concrete discipline. Basically all I'm doing is recording something I'm thankful for every hour. It may seem silly and at times the thing I write down are kinda silly but it's actually become something that I look forward to every new hour and a really good reminder of God's relentless love and provision.

Here's yesterday's list:

- 5am - a place to call home
- 6am - family to drink coffee with
- 7am - transportation through the sky
- 8am - best friends
- 9am - unique personalities
- 10am - the privilege of worshipping
- 11am - languages of all kinds
- 12pm - the opportunity to travel
- 1pm - deep relationships
- 2pm - rain!!
- 3pm - food on the table
- 4pm - protection from the weather
- 5pm - a job where I can love people
- 6pm - chocolate covered items

- 7pm - good and Godly mentors
- 8pm - human diversity
- 9pm - good tunes
- 10pm - time to rest

If any of you wanna join me in this, I think it'd be fun to do together."

How awesome is that? Imagine being thankful every single hour of the day!

Gratitude really does help to rewire your brain for more positive experiences and it improves your outlook on life, setting you up for a more successful deconstruction process.

To put all of this to the test, I've incorporated this gratitude exercise into my 90-day Square 1 course for people who are deconstructing their faith. For an entire week, everyone is encouraged to spend the day practicing some form of gratitude like writing a letter to someone they're grateful for, setting an hourly alarm to keep a list like the one above, calling someone on the phone to express gratitude, or other methods such as these.

The results? Better than we could have imagined. Everyone who took the time to practice gratitude on a daily basis for 7 days in a row experienced freedom from negative thoughts, greater joy, increased happiness and even a more positive attitude about bad things that happened to them during the week.

So, our brains either help us or hurt us when it comes to rethinking our beliefs. If we hang on to old ways of thinking, it can hold us back from real growth. If we allow ourselves to be trapped in an endless toxic feedback loop, we'll find ourselves experiencing unhealthy stress and anxiety that can lead to serious health problems. But, if we can rewire our brains to celebrate all the good things around us, we'll discover an ability to experience joy and to thrive in ways we never thought possible.

Our brains can be the key to unlocking the unlimited potential of profound spiritual experiences with the Divine. Especially if we're willing to let go of our certainty to embrace the beautiful mystery that lies outside of our limited ways of knowing from an informational perspective, and as we press in deeper to uncover the unlimited ways of knowing from an experiential aspect.

From *episteme* to *ginosko*; information to transformation, the ways we approach knowing God can radically impact our experience of God, or the lack thereof.

The Problem With Problem Solving

Another fascinating thing about our brains is how they are wired to detect patterns and find meaning. We simplify our complex visual reality using the principles of Gestalt Psychology, for example, to make sense of our surroundings. We tend to group objects by proximity and similarity, perceive objects in terms of continuity and symmetry, and create meaning in terms of assumed closure and common fate, according to psychologists who have studied the way humans process visual information.

PROXIMITY

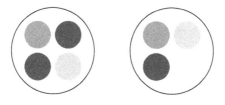

The Gestalt Law of Proximity says that our brains group things that are near one another.

SIMILARITY

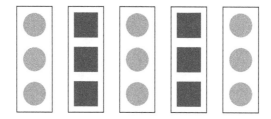

Unless those objects are significantly different, in which case we will group them by similarity.

CONTINUITY

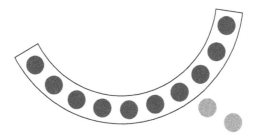

Because of the Law of Continuity, we will assume that the smoother path is the correct path to follow.

SIMPLICITY (PRAGNANZ)

But, if those curves overlap, we'll tend to see those shapes in their simplest forms.

SYMMETRY

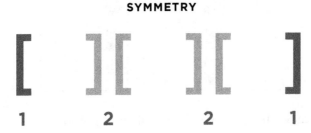

Our brains also prefer symmetry, which is why we do not visually group the shapes above in terms of 1-2-2-1

but in terms of 2-2-2 as we see in the image above. Our brains group these objects into sets automatically.

CLOSURE

The Law of Closure is why we see an implied shape in the above image, even though it is not actually there.

COMMON FATE

The Law of Common Fate says that if a group of objects move together, we assume they move as one object, even though they are clearly six separate objects.

What's so fascinating about these Gestalt Laws of Psychology is that we all do these things automatically because this is the way our brains are wired to process information, group objects visually, and find patterns in our surrounding world.

We also tend to see patterns and interpret random shapes as faces, or objects as well. This is why you can see the face of Abraham Lincoln in that bathroom tile, or why we see elephants in the clouds, or even why that funny place on your ceiling looks like a dog riding a dinosaur. Because our brains are wired to look for meaning and to find patterns in things—even if those patterns aren't actually saying or communicating anything at all.

In fact, it's precisely because our brains are wired to seek for meaning and look for patterns that we are so attracted to mystery. Our brains love a puzzle we can solve. We love questions we can discover the answers to. We are fascinated by riddles, and intrigued by the unknown. This is why so many of us become obsessed with UFOs, or Sasquatch, or the Loch Ness Monster.

In general, this obsession with mystery is a good thing. It keeps us thinking, it stimulates our mind, and it can even, potentially, lead us to abandon outdated ideas in favor of new concepts that lead us into greater freedom, or a better life, or even deeper wisdom and maturity. At its best, embracing mystery can create a spiritual vortex that draws us close to the center of ultimate Truth, like a cosmic magnet pulling us inevitably into a deeper connection with the Divine that transcends knowledge and expands our ability to rest in the presence of the endlessly captivating unknown.

But, at its worst, our desire to find answers and solve mysteries can also lead us away from the place where we are in awe of all we do not know, and into a false sense of certainty about what we become convinced is "the answer."

As long as we can maintain a loose hold on Truth and allow ourselves to sink deeper into the endless deep of an infinite God, we're on the right track. But, once we arrive at the solution; once we believe we have achieved our goal, our fascination with the beautiful mystery is done and we begin to shift our energies into defending our rightness and opposing those who disagree with us.

If we're not very careful, our built-in desire to explore the beautiful mysteries of God can be hijacked whenever we trade the infinite joy of child-like wonder for the false comfort of knowing all the answers.

But, even if we find ourselves mired in the quicksand of certainty, what, if anything, can we truly say we know for sure?

That's worth exploring in our next chapter.

Chapter 6

WHAT DO WE REALLY KNOW?

"All of our knowledge brings us nearer to our ignorance."
T.S. ELIOT

Where would we be today with the Internet? Most of us couldn't find our way around our own towns without Google Maps, or remember our best friend's birthday without those daily Facebook reminders. We've become so dependent upon this World Wide Web that life before this technology seems almost archaic by comparison, and we're only talking about the early Nineties here.

But, what if I told you that there has always been a worldwide communication network where information could be shared and connections could be established across hundreds or even thousands of miles without electricity, smart phones or cell towers? No, I'm not talking about the postal service or the printing press. I'm talking about a global communications network that has been around for millions of years and was only discovered in the 19th century by a German biologist named Albert Frank.

Curious? I hope so. That's sort of the point of this book, isn't it? To rekindle our curiosity and awaken our human capacity for wonder and awe. So, now that I have your attention, what *is* this highly advanced global communications network I'm referring to? Well, it's something that one author has termed "The Wood Wide Web" because it's a clever way to describe the mind-bending communication methods used by trees and fungi as part of Earth's natural internet.[15]

What biologist Albert Frank discovered was a fascinating symbiotic relationship between the roots of trees and plants with fungal colonies that grow around them. He described this phenomenon as "mycorrhiza" and today we now know that roughly 90 percent of all land-based plants are connected to this vast communications network.

It's no surprise that fungi aids in plant growth and contributes to the health of trees and forests. We've known since the 1960's that mushrooms help plants locate water sources and even provide essential nutrients through the mycelia strands around their root systems. They can also protect trees and other plants from disease "by providing counteractive compounds stored in their roots which are triggered when plants are attacked."[16] In return, plants feed their fungi friends a diet of nutritious carbohydrates which they need to thrive.

But protection from disease isn't the only thing this network offers. It also allows trees and plants to communicate with one another in ways that are startlingly similar to the way the US Department of Defense's ARPANET operates (an early version of the internet we have today). Some scientists have even compared this vast tree/fungi network to our own human nervous systems.

---

15 As reported by Philip Perry at BigThink.com in his article "Plants and Trees Communicate Through an Unseen Web", August 25, 2016. https://bigthink.com/surprising-science/plants-and-trees-communicate-help-each-other-and-even-poison-enemies-through-an-unseen-web/?fbclid=IwAR3xnESsYARaIEqPYDaLJExfruy3BBhJwfVBsfWcxK0su1Zl48LpXg2UH1o

16 Ibid.

As an example of how this "Wood Wide Web" works, studies in 1983 proved that different trees used this network to warn each other about invasive insects. "When one tree becomes infested, it warns others who begin producing anti-insect chemicals, to protect against attack. These signals are sent through the air … .since the late 90's however, researchers have proven that trees transfer carbon, nitrogen, phosphorus, and other nutrients, back and forth via mycelia … " and that "when infected with blight, tomato plants release a chemical signal to warn others nearby. These plants also 'eavesdrop' on neighbors, to determine when to build up their defenses against oncoming pathogens … " and "a 2013 study found that broad beans also signaled neighbors through the fungal network, this time due to an aphid infestation."[17]

So, we were not the first biological species to develop a global communications network that allows us to communicate information, share gossip about our neighbors, and respond to the world around us. We just added emojis and cat videos.

How Do We Know What We Know?

As we've already touched on previously in our discussion about the strange phenomenon of the Placebo Effect, it's possible to trick our brains into believing things that are not true and constructing a false reality that we readily accept as true. But what about all the other ways that our perceptions of reality can become fuzzy? What, if anything, can we truly say we know about what we think we know?

---

17 Ibid.

We might think that we can trust our own memories. After all, we experienced it, we lived through it, so therefore, our memories must be trustworthy. Right? Well, maybe not. As some scientists and psychologists have recently discovered, many of our own memories may be manufactured by our brains and even edited over time.

For example, think of one of your most treasured childhood memories. Close your eyes and play the memory over again in your mind right now if you can. Can you see yourself in that memory? Can you recall what you were doing, what you were wearing, what the weather was like? All those details add up to convince you that what you're remembering is an actual snapshot of exactly what happened. But, it's not. In fact, one of the easiest ways to prove that your memory is not an exact snapshot of what actually happened is the fact that you can see yourself in the memory. Because if you can see yourself doing things in your mind's eye, then that means you're watching a movie created by your brain about the memory, not the actual memory itself. Think about it. If you were remembering the actual events, then everything would in the first person. You'd see your own hands and feet, but not yourself from the outside like an observer with a camera. But this isn't the only way to determine whether or not your memories are real or imagined. However, before we get into that, let's first take some time to understand how memories work.

Most people believe that memories are like a recording device that captures an event in the mind so it can be played back later to recover information, answer questions or establish the facts about what happened at that time and in that place. But, decades of psychological studies have revealed to the truth: that memory just doesn't work this way at all. In fact, memory is something we recreate in our imaginations and it's less like a video camera filming reality and more like a Wikipedia page that you—and others—can edit and update over time. That's right, other people can edit your memories in ways you may not even be aware of.

For example, one psychologist who studies memory, Dr. Elizabeth Loftus, discovered that she could influence what subjects remembered after watching films of car accidents by selecting certain words and phrases used in the questions she asked them. If she asked subjects to estimate how fast the cars were traveling when they "hit each other" the numbers were much lower than if she asked them to guess how fast the vehicles were going "when they smashed into each other." Additionally, those who were asked about the vehicles "smashing into each other" reported seeing glass on the ground when there was no glass.

In another study, Dr. Loftus showed another film to subjects where a car ran a stop sign and caused an accident. By asking a series of leading questions, she managed to convince people that what they remembered wasn't a stop sign, but a yield sign.[18]

But it doesn't end there. Loftus also published a study in 2013 involving U.S. soldiers who were undergoing Survival School training and being subjected to mock-interrogations that lasted over half an hour. Afterwards, she was able to convince many of these soldiers that the person who harassed them for those thirty awful minutes was a completely different person who looked nothing like the actual interrogator.[19]

These studies done by Dr. Loftus inspired other psychologists to perform their own experiments with editing and planting false

[18] "How Memory Plays Us" Elizabeth Loftus at TEDxOrangeCoast, Oct. 16, 2013. https://www.youtube.com/watch?v=FMkZWXDulA4

[19] Ibid.

memories in their subjects, with great success. One study in Tennessee convinced over a third of their subjects that they had memories of nearly drowning as a small child and needed to be rescued by a lifeguard. Another study in Canada convinced over half of their subjects that they had survived being attacked by a wild animal in their childhood. Researchers in Italy also convinced people that they had memories of witnessing a demonic possession as a child.[20]

Simply put, our memory is malleable and all-too easily manipulated by our own minds, as well as by outside forces. Therefore, our memory is essentially unreliable as a tool to determine what is real and what isn't.

Not only this, but it's more than possible that the memories we cherish the most—the ones that make us feel good about ourselves, our childhood, our experiences—are almost certainly either fabrications at worse, or distortions of reality at best. We simply cannot trust our memories to give us an accurate picture of what's real, or even to tell us who we are and where we've come from.

If we can't trust our memories to inform us about reality, can we trust our brains to know what's true and what isn't? Maybe not.

How We Hallucinate Conscious Reality

Amil Seth, a professor of Cognitive and Computational Neuroscience at the University of Sussex, England has studied human consciousness for many years and published over 100 scientific papers on the topic. His research suggests that "our conscious experiences of the world around us and of ourselves within it, are a kind of controlled

---

20 Ibid.

hallucination that happen with, through and because of our living bodies."[21]

To start with, we have to try to define what consciousness is and what we mean when we talk about human consciousness. At a basic level, consciousness can be understood as the way we experience the world around us and the way we experience what it means to be ourselves. According to Seth, this experience of self is "probably the aspect of consciousness we all cling to most tightly."[22]

If we start with the ways we experience and understand the world around us, we have to start with our brains because this is the primary organ responsible for receiving and processing sensory data about the world around us. Sights, smells, sounds, textures, temperature, pleasure, pain, and suffering are all processed through our sensory organs by the brain. "Imagine … you are trapped inside a bony skull trying to figure what's out there in the world," says Seth. "There are no lights inside the skull. There's no sound either. All you've got to go on are streams of electrical impulses which are only indirectly related to things in the world, whatever they may be."[23]

Our brain's ability to experience the world around us is also severely limited by our sensory organs because we now know—using sensitive scientific instruments—that the full spectrum of light is far greater than the limited range of light our eyes can perceive. Whereas the human eye can see the ROYGBIV frequencies of light—Red, Orange, Yellow, Green, Blue, Indigo and Violet—otherwise known

---

21 From "Your Brain Hallucinates Your Conscious Reality" by Anil Seth, TED Talk, July 18, 2017: https://www.youtube.com/watch?v=lyu7v7nWzfo

22 Ibid.

23 Ibid.

as the range of Visible Light. But the entire electromagnetic spectrum includes wavelengths of light we cannot perceive such as Ultraviolet, Infrared, Gamma, X-Ray, Microwaves, and Radio waves.

WAVELENGTH (M)

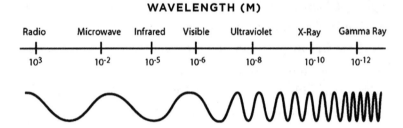

Radio	Microwave	Infrared	Visible	Ultraviolet	X-Ray	Gamma Ray
10^3	10^{-2}	10^{-5}	10^{-6}	10^{-8}	10^{-10}	10^{-12}

What this means is that our eyes are only capable of seeing a very small fraction of the light that is all around us, all the time. There are colors, patterns, and nuances to reality as it is illuminated by this full light spectrum that we are oblivious to. So, what we can see with our eyes isn't all there is to see. In fact, there is more to see than our eyes can possibly perceive or process.

The way our eyes work is fascinating. Light enters the eye through the pupil and strikes receptors at the back of the inside of the eye known as rods and cones. Rods only detect the intensity [brightness or darkness] of the light, but our cone cells measure the frequencies of light received as either red, green, blue, or combinations of those three. Since our cones are only sensitive to red, green or blue, other colors that enter the eye—say yellow for example—this actives both the red and green cone cells so our brain sees that color. The same is true when a light blue wavelength enters the eye—the color cyan—we combine the green and blue receptors to send that signal to the brain. Following this pattern, a wavelength that falls between the blue and red cones should produce green, but it doesn't. Instead, our eyes somehow perceive this as the color magenta. In fact, there is no actual wavelength in the visible spectrum of light that corresponds to magenta. Our brains simply invent this color. That's right. Even though magenta is one of the primary pigment colors we use to create every other color along the visible spectrum, (for example, in the color printing process), it doesn't have an actual wavelength associated to it. It is completely invented in our brains.

So, when we see the color magenta, we are experiencing a phenomenon that does not correspond to reality. We're seeing a color that only exists inside our heads, not a color that appears on the actual spectrum of visible light.

At the same time, there is an entire world of sound that exists outside of our ability to hear. Our ears can only detect sound waves within a certain, narrow bandwidth compared to all that is actually out there to be experienced beyond the audible range.

For example, humans cannot hear below 20Hz, or above 20,000 Hz. There are inaudible Ultra-sounds that dogs, dolphins and bats can hear at the high end, and inaudible Infra-sounds that are too low for our ears, but are detectible by elephants and whales.

So, there is a wider spectrum of light that our eyes cannot see, and a larger range of sound that we cannot hear. It's all out there; it's going on all around us, but it's an aspect of reality that we are largely incapable of experiencing without technological assistance.

This means, our ability to experience the world around us as it actually exists is extremely limited. It also means that our brain's limited perception creates an incomplete picture of what is real and what is not. As Seth puts is, "Our perception—figuring out what's there—[is] a process of informed guesswork. The brain combines these sensory signals with its prior expectations or beliefs about the way the world is to form its best guess of what caused those signals."[24]

Optical illusions are a great way to illustrate how our brains can perceive reality in ways that are not true. For example, if you look at this image below you'll perceive two different shades of gray when, in fact, both blocks are the very same shade of gray. You can prove this to yourself by placing your finger across the center and when you do you'll now perceive that both blocks are the same.

What's happening here? Well, as Seth explains, "The brain is using its prior expectations, built deeply into the circuits of the visual cortex, that a cast shadow dims the appearance of a surface so that we see [one block] as lighter than it really is."[25]

---

24 Ibid.

25 Ibid.

Our brains can also misperceive soundwaves in the very same way. For example, there are several viral videos online where a sound is played and, depending on which word you are focused on, you will either hear "Green Needle" or "Brainstorm." In other words, even though the sound wave never changes, your perception does.

The brain's ability to be fooled, or tricked, into perceiving—misperceiving—reality based on the way it processes sensory information is an indication that we don't always know what is real and what isn't. What we perceive is what our brains tell us to believe, and often, what our brains tell us to perceive is based on its best guess about what might be going on around us.

This changes everything. Rather than reality and perception being an accurate picture of what's going on in the outside world, what we see is that reality and perception are mostly created inside of our brain and projected onto our conception of reality. "We don't just passively perceive the world," Seth concludes, "we actively generate it. The world we experience comes as much, if not more, from the inside out as from the outside in."[26]

It might also come as a shock, but researchers have also found that our experiences of our individual self are also a controlled hallucination generated by our brains. "How can I be deceived about what it means to be me?" one might ask. Well, in much the same way as we hallucinate the world around us, we also hallucinate much of what it means to be an individual self. "The basic background experience of being a unified self is a rather fragile construction of the brain," says Seth.[27] But, as he is quick to remind us, "These are

---

26 Ibid.

27 Ibid.

fundamental changes in how we understand ourselves, but I think they should be celebrated. From a greater sense of understanding comes a greater sense of wonder, and a greater realization that we are part of, not apart from, the rest of nature."[28]

Historical Fiction

One of my favorite short stories was in an anthology of science fiction that my mom bought for me when I was a teenager. The main story I loved in this collection was one that was written as if it were a personal letter between two men in the year 2415 who are debating the veracity of World History (specifically the details of World War 2) based on several details that—for at least one of those men—simply couldn't be true because "they had a cute habit of giving names to their characters that fitted the parts they played in the plots … [and] it is precisely this fictional method of applying names that dismays me when I see the obvious evidences of it in our so-called American history, and thus I am led to the conclusion that what so many of us regard as history is not history at all but pure romancing by flag-waving minstrels."[29]

What follows is a systematic critique of what this higher critic sees as proof that American History, as it has been passed down to everyone, cannot be believed as literal truth. As he explains it, World War II was " … a terrific conflict, so the story goes, [which] resulted in the victory of right over wrong, of decency over tyranny … there was a big bad wolf in this fairytale named Adolph Hitler, a German

---

28 Ibid.

29 From the short story, "Letter From A Higher Critic" by Stewart Robb, as published in *Analog 6*, edited by John W. Campbell, page 261.

ogre who burned people alive in ovens by the millions and who nearly conquered the world! Now, don't you think whoever made up this part of the yarn knew that the name Adolph in Old High German means "Wolf Prince"? And isn't it a coincidence that he descended like a wolf on the fold of those innocent sheep nations ... the name is a fancy of poets, surely!"[30]

As the writer continues, one cannot take the rest of the story seriously because France was saved by a man named "De Gaulle" (which means "Of France") who fights on against all odds to become the eventual leader of France. He also notes that the Russian characters in this fairy tale were named Stalin (which means "Steel") and his sidekick Molotov (which means "Hammer"), and combined these two names are obviously selected because they symbolize the Hammer and Sickle which were national symbols of the Communist party. Finally, he points out that the British leader, Churchill's name evoked a sense of unshakable faith (literally "Church on the Hill") and "was clearly chosen for its positive, spiritual sound."[31]

Of course, we can't leave out the fictional character, President Roosevelt, whose name is the Dutch for "Field of Roses"—a name of excellent odor and a man whose speechwriter was named Rosenman, or literally, "The Rose Man", " ... a gardener who takes care of the flowers of speech from the Field of Roses."[32]

One of the most convincing sections of this faux letter from the future is this part where the skeptical historian points out yet another curious coincidence where, as he says,

---

30 bid.

31 Ibid.

32 Ibid., pg. 262

"they borrowed a still earlier so-called historical event, reversed it to disguise the source and applied it to the Great War. In 1066 it was fabled and generally believed, Normandy invaded England. At the head of the invading troops ... was a minstrel-warrior named Taillefer ... so, our later day minstrels fabled that just as Normandy had invaded England, England and the Allies had now invaded Normandy. And to the leader of the conquering forces the poet historians gave the same name of Taillefer, only this time they translated it first into German— 'Eisenhower'. Both names, as you are aware, mean "Iron-Hewer," a most fitting name for men of war!"[33]

Now, at this point in the story I had to look away from the book and try to comprehend what I was reading. Clearly, the story is not seriously attempting to convince us that the events of World War 2 are fictional. Obviously there was a World War II, and Hitler, Roosevelt, Churchill and the rest were real people. Those events are true and they did happen. So, what's going on here? Perhaps the point he's trying to make is just how much human history seems to follow a narrative pattern. Or maybe he wants us to notice how taking such a critical view of coincidental details can distract us from the truth of something? As the author of the letter in this story concludes, "If I could be persuaded to believe this fragrant nonsense, I would have to admit that in these latter days—as you call them—history is falling into some predetermined, divine plan: "towards which all creation moves." But that, alas, I can never believe."[34]

We don't have to look very far to find even stranger coincidences surrounding historical events like this. They're honestly everywhere we look. How often have you heard a true story and marveled at how

---

33 Ibid., pg. 263

34 Ibid., pg. 265

unbelievable some of the details are. You might have even responded by saying, "If I didn't know this was a true story, I wouldn't believe it!" or maybe, "If you made this story up they wouldn't believe you!"

What is real and what is fiction isn't always so clear to us, is it? What we think we know may be something others made up, and the unbelievability of the story isn't always a good barometer for how true things might be.

For example, you may be aware of the bizarre similarities between the assassination of Abraham Lincoln and John F. Kennedy. The more you start to dig into it, the more impossible some of the coincidences seem to be. Here are a few of the more surprising connections between the two men:

- Both were elected to congress is '46: Lincoln in 8146 and Kennedy in 1946

- Both were elected President in '60: Lincoln in 1860 and Kenney in 1960

- Both were concerned about civil rights: Lincoln wrote the Emancipation Proclamation to free the slaves and Kennedy was the first to propose the Civils Rights Act.

- Both married in their 30's to women in their 20's.

- Both lost a son while in the White House: Lincoln's son William, and Kennedy's infant son Patrick.

- Both were shot on a Friday, in the head, in the presence of their wives by Southerners.

- Both were succeeded by Southerners named Johnson: Andrew John [Lincoln] and Lyndon Johnson [Kennedy].

- Both successors were born in '08: Andrew Johnson in 1808 and Lyndon Johnson in 1908.

- Lincoln was shot at Ford's theater. Kennedy was shot in a Ford, Lincoln limousine.

- Both assassins were killed before they could face trial.

- Lincoln's assassin ran from a theater and Kennedy's assassin was captured in a theater.

After examining these details, it's almost too much for us to believe. How could there be so many similarities between the two Presidents? Wouldn't you doubt the truth of a such stories if these names were changed?

Here's what I'm trying to suggest by sharing all of this: *We can't always know what's true and what isn't.* Just because something seems true doesn't mean it is true. Just because something seems false doesn't mean it's false. Our ability to know what is, or what is not true is often extremely difficult to verify. As we've seen so far, we cannot trust our brains, or our own memories, or even what we see with our eyes or hear with our own ears. The truth, and the world around us, is more wondrous, strange and perplexing than we can possibly imagine: Trees communicate. Memories fluctuate. Reality itself might be something we hallucinate.

How can anyone possibly say they "know" almost anything is true? Especially when it comes to a being so magnificent, marvelous, complex and unimaginably vast as what we imagine when we talk about an eternal God.

This is why it's such a bad idea to allow our theology to be defined as having the right information about God. Our ability to know things is already in doubt. What we know and how we know it are under constant revision and suspicion. The truth is that none of us can trust the veracity of our information. Besides, we already realize that knowing God has nothing to do with *what* we know, and so much more to do with *who* we know … and that knowing is based on experiences that transcend sensory data. In the same way we cannot measure or quantify or prove how much we love our spouse or our children. We nevertheless know this love is real.

Exploring Ideaspace

Historians have noted a strange phenomenon that some call "The Law of Dual Discovery" or "The Multiple Independent Discovery Effect." This is a term used to describe the tendency for certain discoveries to have more than one source, even when separated by thousands of miles, without interaction or communication of any kind.

One of the first comprehensive lists of multiples was put together by William Ogburn and Dorothy Thomas, in 1922, and they found 148 major scientific discoveries that fit this multiple, or dual discovery pattern.[35]

In fact, over the years it has become so commonplace for independent multiple discoveries to take place, several Nobel laureates are commonly announced in physics, chemistry, physiology, medicine and economics; because there are sometimes two, or even three, different people who have all documented the same discoveries simultaneously.

A few more examples of Dual Discovery include:

- Independent formulation of Calculus (17th Century) by Isaac Newton, Gottfried Wilhelm Leibniz and others, described by A. Rupert Hall.

---

35 As reported in *The New Yorker* magazine article, "In The Air" by Malcolm Gladwell, May 5, 2008: https://www.newyorker.com/magazine/2008/05/12/in-the-air

- The Law of the Conservation of Energy was formulated 4 times independently in 1847 by Joule, Thomson, Colding and Helmholz.

- Multiple discovery of Oxygen (18th Century) by Carl Wilhelm Scheele, Joseph Priestley, Antoine Lavoisier and others.

- Theory of Evolution (19th Century) by Charles Darwin and Alfred Russel Wallace.

- The Blast Furnace (invented independently in China, Europe and Africa).

- The Crossbow (invented independently in China, Greece, Africa, northern Canada, and the Baltic countries).

- Magnetism (discovered independently in Greece, China, and India)

The list goes on: "Three different mathematicians invented decimal fractions. Color photography was invented at the same time by two different men: Charles Cros and also Louis Ducos du Hauron. Logarithms were invented by John Napier and Henry Briggs (Britain), and by Joost Bürgi (Switzerland). In 1611 there were four independent discoveries of sunspots by Galileo (Italy), Scheiner (Germany), Fabricius (Holland) and Harriott (England) … .There seem to have been at least six different inventors of the thermometer and no less than nine claimants of the invention of the telescope. Typewriting machines were invented simultaneously in England and in America by several individuals in these countries. The steamboat is claimed as the 'exclusive' discovery of Fulton, Jouffroy, Rumsey, Stevens and Symmington."[36]

What Ogburn and Thomas surmised as they compiled their first dizzying list of Multiple Discoveries was that scientific discoveries must be inevitable. As if some unseen force was either guiding the timing of these discoveries for humanity's benefit.

However, later theories began to emerge to suggest an even more fantastic possibility. Something called *Ideaspace*.

What is it? Well, as suggested by science fiction author Rudy Rucker's essay, "Life As A Fractal In Hilbert Space," *Ideaspace* is a dimension of ideas that exists outside of our waking reality but is nevertheless accessible to us through our dreams or imaginations. So, theoretically, the reason why several people at once can experience the same "Eureka!" moment is simply because they have all been tuned in to the *Ideaspace* frequency where this idea originates. Because their antennae were raised and attuned to capture this idea, they have, in a sense, all photographed the same elusive creature in its natural habitat and brought it back with them into this reality to share it with all of us.

Curiously, this theory overlaps quite well with Plato's ideas of an Ideal Form where all material objects and ideals originate from, and especially with Carl Jung's concept of the Collective Unconscious and maybe Hegel's philosophy of the Spirit where humankind is influenced by a sort of deeper magic that originates beyond the confines of conscious realism and refers to shared mental concepts, instincts and archetypes.

---

36 Ibid.

As Jung understood it, the Collective Unconscious has a profound influence on our daily lives in ways most of us are not aware of; an influence that involves symbols that we tend to clothe in meaning and respond to unconsciously. There is also the suggestion by some theorists that this same Collective Unconscious might be an actual dimension of reality that lies alongside our own waking reality that we access through our dreams as we sleep.

Plato believed that the physical world was not as real or as true as the absolute, unchangeable and eternal realm of ideas. Jung's theory of the Collective Unconscious took that even further. As Jung explained it:

> "The essential thing, psychologically, is that in dreams, fantasies, and other exceptional states of mind the most far-fetched mythological motifs and symbols can appear indigenously at any time, often, apparently, as the result of particular influences, traditions, and excitations working on the individual, but more often without any sign of them. These "primordial images" or "archetypes," as I have called them, belong to the basic stock of the unconscious psyche and cannot be explained as personal acquisitions. Together they make up that psychic stratum which has been called the collective unconscious." [37]

> "The existence of the collective unconscious means that individual consciousness is anything but a tabula rasa [blank slate] and is not immune to predetermining influences ... The collective unconscious comprises in itself the psychic life of our ancestors right back to the earliest beginnings. It is the matrix of all conscious psychic occurrences, and hence it exerts an influence that compromises the

---

37 "The Significance of Constitution and Heredity in Psychology" (November 1929), pg. 112

freedom of consciousness in the highest degree, since it is continually striving to lead all conscious processes back into the old paths."[38]

"In addition to our immediate consciousness, which is of a thoroughly personal nature and which we believe to be the only empirical psyche ... *there exists a second psychic system of a collective, universal, and impersonal nature which is identical in all individuals. This collective unconscious does not develop individually but is inherited. It consists of pre-existent forms, the archetypes, which can only become conscious secondarily and which give definite form to certain psychic contents.*" [emphasis mine][39]

At any rate, the concept of an *Ideaspace* where all ideas originate, and which some of us can access through various means of sensing or perception, is one possible way of understanding why so many different people, in so many different places, have all made the same discoveries in math, science, chemistry, art and music at the same time.

Musician Jean Baptiste explains his experiences tapping into this creative space in similar terms when he goes on stage to perform a 90-minute show that's completely improvised:

"There's something very transcendent about allowing yourself to be a vessel in the moment for the music that's always in the air—it's always there ... it's a current, and you can dip into the stream—the stream of conscious. We can do it in our dreams, with our thoughts, but to do that with music is terrifying but ... it can [also] be a way to give that

---

38 Ibid.

39 From Carl Jung's lecture, "The Concept of the Collective Unconscious" to the Abernethian Society at St. Bartholomew's Hospital in London, Oct. 19, 1936

[as a gift] to the audience so when they leave they can live without judgement, and live free and truly exist."[40]

When we open ourselves up to this creative force and let go of our expectations, setting aside our egos to simply respond to the rhythm of Divine imagination as it flows into our minds and through our being, we capture a glimpse of that mystery that surrounds everyone and everything.

This is what it probably looks like to dance with God, or to collaborate with the Spirit of Truth.

Does all of this cause you to wonder? Are you curious about where ideas really come from? Could there be something to this theory of a collective unconscious that drives human creativity and development? Could we call that shared consciousness "God"?

What if there were scientific discoveries that suggested exactly this? Wouldn't you want to know about that? I know I would.

That's what we'll talk about in our next chapter.

---

40 From *The Late Show* with Stephen Colbert, February 22, 2022: https://www.youtube.com/watch?v=RM8kA5Q3Lyc

Chapter 7

QUANTUM THEOLOGY

*"Sometimes well-formed questions are more
useful than well-formed answers."*

ANONYMOUS[41]

Way back in 1801, a scientist by the name of Thomas Young wanted to answer the question: "Is light made of waves or particles?" The debate about the nature of light was one that had confounded physicists for many years and he wanted to settle the issue once and for all.

Not only did Young *not* answer this question, he inadvertently set off a wildfire of even more questions that scientists didn't even know they could, or should, be asking; not only about the nature of light, but about reality itself.

But, let's not get ahead of ourselves. First, let's explain the experiment and how Young approached the problem of whether or not light was composed of waves or particles. What Young surmised was that if light was made of waves, it would create a certain distinguishable pattern as it passed through a pair of slits cut into a plate on its way

---

41 Quoted from a poster for Graduate Studies in Fiber at Cranbrook
    Academy of Art I stole from the Art Department at UTEP
    around 1988 or 1989 that now hangs in my office.

to a light-sensitive screen on the other side. Or, if made of particles, then light would create a different pattern on the same screen as it passed through the double slits. Either way, the pattern on the other side would reveal the nature of light as either waves or particles. After aiming a beam of light at the plate with the double-slits, what Young found was that light was indeed a wave. The interference pattern on the other side was consistent with the way waves behaved under similar conditions. Case closed. Or, so he thought.

As technology advanced over the next 100 years, scientists had the ability to fire individual photons of light at the plate, and to measure which of the two slits the photon passed through. That's when things started to get interesting. Because, if detectors were placed at the slits, the photon suddenly started to behave like a particle, not a wave. When detectors were removed—or when no one was watching—the photons went back to behaving like waves. In other words, it was as if the photons knew whether they were being watched and behaved differently if they were than if they were not. So, if not observed, the photon passed through both slits at once—like a wave. If observed, the photons passed through only one of the two slits. What was going on?

Well, to answer that question, physicists created an entire field of study known as Quantum Mechanics. As famed physicist Richard Feynman put it, "[The double-slit experiment] is a phenomenon which is impossible to explain in any classical way. In reality, it contains the only mystery of quantum mechanics."[42] In fact, he was also fond of

---

42 Feynman, Richard P.; Robert B. Leighton; Matthew Sands (1965). *The Feynman Lectures on Physics*, Vol. 3. Addison-Wesley. pp. 1.1–1.8.

saying that "all of quantum mechanics could be gleaned from carefully thinking through the implications of this single experiment."[43]

Soon, it was discovered that electrons and other atomic-scale entities, including molecules, also behaved in this strange way when subjected to the double-slit experiment: as a particle when observed, and as a wave if not observed. In fact, it was impossible to observe any object as both a wave and a particle at the same time. Depending on the methods used, the object could be one, or the other, but never both.

So, without going to deep down that rabbit hole, let's stop and consider the implications of this now-infamous double-slit experiment, especially on the way photons behave. Are the photons sentient? Are they aware they are being watched? How does the mere act of observation change the behavior of these supposedly non-living things? Honestly, we don't exactly know the answer. Somehow, whenever a conscious person observes an object, something changes. What that suggests is that there is an ineffable connection between consciousness and matter.

But wait, it gets weirder. Physicists have also found that sub-atomic particles exhibit properties of Quantum Entanglement. This is a physical phenomenon where groups of particles interact and share special proximity in a way such that the quantum state of each particle within the group cannot be described independently of the state of the other particles—even when those particles are separated by a large distance.

This effect is at the heart of the disparity between Classical Physics and Quantum Physics and gives rise to seemingly paradoxical properties

43 Greene, Brian (1999). *The Elegant Universe: Super Strings, Hidden Dimensions, and the Quest for the Ultimate Theory.* New York: W.W. Norton. pp. 97–109

since any measurement of a particle results in an irreversible wave function collapse of that particle and changes its original quantum state, affecting the entire entangled system.

What's even more perplexing is that Quantum Entanglement has been demonstrated with photons, neutrinos, electrons, large molecules and even small diamonds.

At this point you may be asking yourself, "Okay, but what does any of this mean?" Well, according to Quantum Entanglement, individual particles are not truly separate from the whole. In other words: everything is connected. And, according to Quantum Physics, observation changes the way particles behave. In other words: consciousness impacts the material world.

Or, as famed Physicist, Sir James Jeans explained it:

"The stream of knowledge is heading towards a non-mechanical [non material] reality; the Universe begins to look more and more like a great thought than like a great machine. Mind no longer appears to be an accidental intruder into the realm of matter … we ought rather hail it as the creator and governor of the realm of matter."[44]

These are huge implications, especially from a spiritual or theological perspective. *Everything is connected. Consciousness influences reality.*

This startling overlap between science and spirituality is fascinating stuff. Yet, it challenges both the scientist and the theologian to abandon some of their most precious assumptions to see the truth. As Dr. Amit Goswami, a physics professor at the Institute of Theoretical Sciences at the University of Oregon explains:

------

44 *The Mysterious Universe*, by Sir James Jean, p. 137

"Today, in physics, we face a great dilemma. In quantum physics—the new physics—we have found a theoretical framework that works; it explains myriad laboratory experiments and more ... Yet we cannot make sense of the mathematics of quantum physics without suggesting an interpretation of experimental results that many people can only look upon as paradoxical, even impossible. Behold the following quantum properties:

- A quantum object can be at more than one place at the same time.

- A quantum object cannot be said to manifest in ordinary space-time reality until we observe it as a particle.

- A quantum object ceases to exist here and simultaneously appears in our existence over there, [although] we cannot say it went through the intervening space.

- A manifestation of one quantum object, caused by our observation, simultaneously influences its correlated twin object—no matter how far apart they are.

" ... [all] this is a paradox if consciousness is made of atoms [or, if matter is the source of consciousness]. But if we flip our view of what the world is made of, this paradox is very satisfactorily resolved ... suppose all things, including atoms, are made of consciousness, instead! [Therefore, I conclude] the world is made of consciousness. Atoms are made of consciousness."[45]

This, my friends, changes everything. In fact, it challenges the way we look at the world, the universe, ourselves, other people, and the nature of reality itself. As the great Niels Bohr once said: "Those who

---

45 *The Self-Aware Universe* by Amit Goswami, P.H.D., pp 4; 6.

are not shocked when they first come across quantum theory cannot possibly have understood it."

For a few hundred years now scientists and philosophers have debated the answer to the question: "How does consciousness arise from matter?" Assuming a materialist worldview that everything is made of atoms; everything is matter and energy, then the question of consciousness becomes a difficult one to answer. More specifically, the question "Why does consciousness arise in the human brain?" is one that neither philosophers nor scientists have been able to answer from a materialist perspective. But, with these new implications arising from quantum physics, we now realize we've been asking the wrong question all along. It's not "Why does consciousness arise from matter?" it's actually, "How does matter arise from consciousness?" Because, without consciousness, there is no matter. Or, as one theologian phrased it, *"In the beginning the earth was without form and void, and God said, 'Let there be light', and there was light."* Or perhaps you may prefer to say it this way:

> "In the beginning was the Word [Logos], and the Word was with God, and the Word was God. He was in the beginning with God. All things came into being through him, and without him not one thing came into being. What has come into being in him was life, and the life was the light of all people. The light shines in the darkness, and the darkness did not overcome it." (John 1:1-5)

It's not only the Christian theology that affirms these notions. Mystics from all streams of faith throughout the ages have been telling us the spiritual reality is the only true reality; that consciousness and the Eternal Self goes by many names: Atman (Buddhists), The Great Spirit (Native Americans), Brahman (Hindus), Inner Light (Quakers), etc.

What quantum science tells us is that consciousness creates reality. Nothing exists outside of consciousness. Nothing.

"'Recall the uncertainty principle,' says Goswami. 'If the product of the uncertainty in position and the uncertainty in momentum is a constant, then reducing the uncertainty of one measure increases the uncertainty of the other measure. Extrapolating from this argument, we can see that if the position is known with complete certainty, then the momentum becomes completely uncertain. And vice versa. 'But surely,' they say, 'the electron must be somewhere; we just don't know where.' No, it is worse. We cannot even define the position of the electron in ordinary space and time … Can we assign the electron any manifest reality in space and time between observations? According to the Copenhagen interpretation of quantum mechanics, the answer is no … .Between observations, the electron exists as a possibility form, like the Platonic archetype … '"[46]

This calls back to our discussion about *Ideaspace* and Plato's concept of an Archetype realm where all objects exist in perfection prior to our discovery or creation of them. What quantum science is telling us is that this *Ideaspace* reality is, indeed, not only possible but extremely likely to be an accurate expression of how things operate. Our consciousness creates reality. In the quantum reality, things only exist when we observe them.

Now, this can seem pretty far-fetched, I agree. But, based on what we are learning about reality from the quantum realm, it makes sense. As Goswami explains,

"Perhaps the most important, and most insidious, assumption that we absorb in our childhoods is that of the material world of objects existing out there—independent of subjects, who are the observers … Quantum physics says no. When we are not looking [at an object, its] possibility wave spreads, albeit by a miniscule amount. When we look, the wave collapses instantly; thus the wave could not be in

---

46 Ibid., pp 58-59

space-time ... There is no object in space-time without a conscious subject looking at it ... Nothing is outside of consciousness."[47]

So, if things only exist when we observe them, then let's take a moment to consider something perhaps even more astounding: Our brains are quantum systems that constantly observe the outside world. This observation of the world around us literally creates the reality we see and experience. More than this, our brains even perceive ourselves. The very definition of human consciousness is to be self-aware. So, without this self-awareness, would our self even exist at all?

This is a very fascinating question. If things only exist when we observe them, then how do we exist? Perhaps because God is the ultimate and original Observer of all things. We exist because God observes us. God creates us and all reality by simply looking at us.

This is why we can say that Christ holds all things together; and that nothing was made apart from Christ ... and all things exist by him, for him, and through him.

" ... For in him [Christ] all things in heaven and on earth were created, things visible and invisible, whether thrones or dominions or rulers or powers—all things have been created through him and for him. He himself is before all things, and in him all things hold together. He is ... the beginning, the firstborn from the dead, so that he might come to have first place in everything. For in him all the fullness of God was pleased to dwell." (Col. 1:16-19)

Not only was the fullness of God pleased to dwell in Christ, the fullness of Christ was also pleased to come and dwell in us, as it says in Ephesians 1: 23 " ... *we are all filled with the fullness of [Christ] who*

---

47   Ibid., pp 59-60

fills everything in every way" and *" ... we are all one in Christ, Jesus."* (Gal. 3:28)

This is the quantum reality that resolves the paradox of consciousness and matter; energy and spirit; science and theology. Everything is connected. Everything is consciousness.

Isn't it fascinating how this entire field of quantum mechanics originated when scientists attempted to understand the nature of light? Isn't it interesting that Genesis begins by telling us how the Creation began with light?

You might wonder, what does light have to do with us? Well, you might be surprised, actually. New research by Northwestern University researchers, published in the journal Scientific Reports, shows that when a human egg is fertilized, it releases a flash of light. They've actually managed to capture the flash on film which is released when calcium interacts with zinc at the moment of conception and creates light-emitting molecule probes called "zinc sparks."[48]

So, your life and my life began with a flash of light. We are literally born from light. Our brains are quantum systems. We observe ourselves, and our own thoughts, and our world around us. This act of observation, even within our own consciousness, creates our reality and impacts it constantly. We are not separate from our consciousness, and we are not separate from our observation of reality through our consciousness. Simply put, "nothing is outside consciousness."

As Amit Goswami says, "There is another paradoxical way to think of the nonlocal reality—as being both everywhere and nowhere, everywhen and nowhen. This is still paradoxical, but it is suggestive,

---

48 *US News* article, "During Conception, Human Eggs Emit Sparks", by Rachel Dicker, April 26, 2016: https://www.usnews.com/news/articles/2016-04-26/human-eggs-emit-zinc-sparks-at-moment-of-fertilization

isn't it? ... .Nonlocality and transcendence is nowhere and now here."[49] And, as we continue to question the strange behavior of electrons and photons in relation to observation, we must conclude that " ... the electron and other submicroscopic particles ... are, according to the new physics, merely extensions of ourselves."[50]

This realization has led scientists, and mystics alike, to conclude that there is no real division between objects or persons, even if we perceive reality this way at times. The truth is, there is no "us and them" or "this and that", there is only "us" and there is only "this" which is one interconnected reality that cannot be explained, nor denied.

All reality is the result of consciousness. All consciousness is the same consciousness, shared across all conscious reality.

Another way of expressing this phenomenon might be to use the analogy of a large bonfire which endlessly lights every candle that is placed near it. One could light an infinite number of candles from a single fire. Does this mean there are an infinite number of fires? Or is the reality that all flames are the same flame?

Essentially, there is only one consciousness and we Christians refer to this as God or Christ. "Christ is all and is in all," as the Apostle Paul tells us in Colossians 3:11. Christ "abides in us as we abide in Christ", as Jesus affirms in John 15:4. "We are all One in Christ Jesus our Lord," as Paul again confirms in Galatians 3:28.

As Jesus promised us, "One day you will realize that I am in my Father, and you are in me, and I am in you." (John 14:20)

---

49 *The Self-Aware Universe*, by Amit Goswami, pp 61

50 Ibid., pp 77

We are all in God/Christ and God/Christ is in all of us. As scripture affirms over and over again, "God is the One in whom we live and move and have our being." (Acts 17:28)

This means that the mystics were right about our connections to God, the Universe, one another, and every other living [and nonliving] thing in the universe: We are all One in ways that we cannot fully comprehend.

So, whatever I do to you, I do to myself, and to God. Or, as Jesus phrased it: "Whatever you have done to the least of these, you have done it unto me." (See Matt. 25:40)

This gives new insight into the prayer of Jesus in the Gospel of John where he asks the Father to "make us One even as [Christ] and the Father are one." (John 17:21-23)

Think about that for a moment. Just how connected would we have to be to experience the same sort of "Oneness" that Jesus had with the Father? This is more than merely getting along or hanging out together. Much more. Jesus expresses a desire for humanity to experience the exact same transcendent "Oneness" with one another that Jesus and the Father experience: A unity that goes beyond relationship and moves closer to essence and being where we cannot discern where one ends and the other begins.

The great Martin Luther King, Jr. used to explain our connectivity with one another like this:

> "It really boils down to this: that all life is interrelated. We are all caught in an inescapable network of mutuality, tied into a single garment of destiny. Whatever affects one destiny affects all indirectly."

Perhaps, on some level, this is why we are urged to pray for one another? Maybe, in some weird way, whenever I focus on your pain and make it my own, something really does change in the fabric of space/time? By observing you and focusing on your situation, do I have the power to influence the outcome of your struggle in some small way?

On another level, I cannot help but draw analogies to the Trinity when it comes to the way that we are called to love God and love one another. Jesus connects these two things by saying that they are like one another. But how?

Perhaps it works like this: God is Love and when we receive love from God we then share this love with others and as they receive this love and return it back to us, we complete the circle whenever we receive love from them. Think of it like a triangle, with God at the top, ourselves at the bottom left and the other person or persons at the bottom right of the triangle. Whenever love flows freely from God, to us, and from us to others, and then from others back to us and then back to God—in all directions at the same time without interruption—this is when we begin to fully realize—and more importantly to experience—this beautiful connection that exists at all times between us and God and everyone else.

Does any of this make sense? Hopefully, so. The more I meditate on these things, the more convinced I am that we are all sharing the same life, and spirit, and consciousness and that this experience of Christ in us is all that really matters. Separation is an illusion. None of us is, or ever could be, separated from God—the Original Observer who holds us and all reality together. We are quantum beings observing and creating reality all around us. We are children of light who vibrate at the frequency of love and radiate the image of God outward into the universe without end.

Reality is more mysterious than any of us could ever have imagined. There is more to know than we know. Truth is not some external thing outside of ourselves. In fact, if consciousness creates and upholds reality, then truth can only be known through a deeper awareness of—and connection to—consciousness. This is why silence and meditation are so crucial for our spiritual growth and development process.

When we are still, and when we slow down enough to "know" (ginosko) God, who is pure being and consciousness, we are finally ready to experience the Divine Love of God which "transcends knowledge" (information) and is "wider, and longer, and higher, and deeper" than we know, so that we "may be filled to the measure of the fullness of God.")Eph. 3:18-19)

Chapter 8

THE MYSTERY BOX

"Every view is the wrong view when it's held
as the only view that's the true view."

THICH NHAT HANH

Before we move on from Quantum Science, there's one thing I need to point out: even though Theologians and Quantum Scientists are essentially both talking about the same things, it seems like the Scientists are the only ones who are genuinely filled with awe and wonder while the Theologians are anything but.

Why is that? Perhaps because the Theologians are convinced they already have all the answers and the Quantum Scientists are convinced they do not.

This sense of curiosity is what creates the feelings of anticipation surrounding discovery of new ideas for the scientists. Theologians know they are right and defend their certainty. Scientists celebrate being wrong and delight in their ignorance. As scientist and author Carlo Rovelli phrases it, *"This permanent doubt, [is] the deep source of science."*[51]

As we've already seen, however, theologians have no reason to be so certain about God. Especially when their own scriptures remind them of the fact that God is shrouded in mystery:

"*For now* we see as through a glass darkly, *but one day* we will know God face-to-face. *Now, we only know in part,* but soon we will know fully, even as we are fully known." (1 Cor. 13:12, emphasis mine(

"[God] has made everything beautiful and appropriate in its time. He has also *planted eternity [a sense of divine purpose] in the human heart [a mysterious longing which nothing under the sun can satisfy, except God]*—yet man cannot find out (comprehend, grasp) what God has done from the beginning to the end." (Ecclesiastes 3:11 AMP, emphasis mine)

In light of these things, I urge you to nurture your own sense of divine wonder and to cultivate your inner capacity to embrace mystery.

Curiosity may kill the cat, but it gives life to those who seek truth and abide outside the walls of certainty.

In the book *Think Again,* author Adam Grant, shares the story of how one Nobel-Prize-Winning Psychologist, David Kahneman, reacted when it was revealed to him that his assumptions were wrong:

"His eyes lit up, and a huge grin appeared on his face. 'That was wonderful,' he said. 'I was wrong.'

"Later, [when the author sat down with him for lunch and asked him about his reaction] … He said that … he genuinely enjoys discovering that he was wrong, because it means he is now less wrong than he was before."[52]

"' … Being wrong is the only way I feel sure I've learned anything,' he said.

---

52 *Think Again,* by Adam Grant, pp 61.

"When [the author] asked him how he stays in that mode, he said he refuses to let his beliefs become part of his identity … 'My attachment to my ideas is provisional. There's no unconditional love for them.'"[53]

What an astounding perspective to have. It makes me wonder; do I have an unconditional love for my beliefs rather than an unconditional love for a God that defies my Theology? What about my unconditional love for my fellow man? Or do I have unquestionable beliefs that prevent me from having an unconditional love for my neighbor? Are people who disagree with me heretics? False Teachers? Enemies of Christ? Or, are they simply people who think differently—*metanoia*—than I do about a God that none of us can ever fully comprehend?

Professor Richard Conn Henry of John Hopkins University said recently in an article published in Nature—the most prestigious scientific journal in the world—the following:

"One benefit of switching humanity to a correct perception of the world is the resulting joy of discovering the mental nature of the universe. *We have no idea what this mental nature implies, but—the great thing is—it is true. Beyond the acquisition of this perception, physics can no longer help.* You may descend into solipsism, expand to deism, or something else if you can justify it—just don't ask physics for help … *The universe is immaterial. It is mental and spiritual. Live and enjoy.*"[54] [emphasis mine]

Clearly, there is more of our universe to know than we know. And even what we think we know, we cannot fully comprehend. We live in a mysterious universe that is more filled with wonder than we have ever before imagines.

---

53 Ibid., pp 62

54 From the article "The Mental Universe" by R.C. Henry, *Nature Journal*, July 7, 2005, pg. 29

Identity Crisis

One of the barriers many people face when it comes to shifting their paradigms about science, theology or even reality itself is the challenge of separating our beliefs from our personal identity.

As Adam Grant observes in his book, "Who you are should be a question of what you value, not what you believe."[55]

Maybe we've made the mistake of believing that we *are* what we believe? Maybe we need to reassess our identity based on Whose image we are created in, and not on what beliefs we currently hold so dear?

The author of 1 John has a wonderful perspective on how we should approach our identities, and the mystery surrounding these things:

> "Dear friends, now we are children of God, and what we will be has not yet been made known. But we know that when Christ appears, we shall be like him, for we shall see him as he is." (1 John 3:2)

Who are we? The Children of God. What are we being transformed into? The image of Christ. But notice that, even that isn't completely known. It says "what we will be has not yet been made known," which means that even though we can affirm that we will be like Christ, we're still not entirely certain what that really means. And that's wonderful!

There's an interesting parallel passage to this one in 1 Corinthians where Paul wraps up his beautiful chapter on love by reminding us of this:

> "For now we see only a reflection as in a mirror; then we shall see face to face. Now I know in part; then I shall know fully, even as I am fully known." (v. 12)

---

55 Ibid.

What we see and know now is only a pale reflection in a mirror, but one day we will see God and "know fully" the majesty and beauty and glory of God as the veil is removed. For now, however, we only "know in part" and, once again, this is wonderful. Why? Because it means that there is more of Christ to known than anyone can ever know on this side of the grave. The best is yet to come.

What's Inside?

J.J. Abrams, the television and film director who co-created the series, *LOST*, and brought us films like *Cloverfield, Super 8,* and the re-booted *Star Trek* films, has something wonderful to tell us about the power of embracing mystery.

Abrams loves to tell the story of how his Grandfather took him, when he was a young boy, to a magic shop and told him to pick out anything he wanted. He looked around the shop with eyes full of wonder at all of the amazing illusions, top hats, magic wands, secret boxes with hidden compartments, and so much more. After a few minutes he finally found what he wanted. It was a large box, covered in a large black question mark. It was called *The Magic Mystery Box.* "It was $50 worth of magic tricks for only $15," he says, "which is a savings."

More than 30 years later, Abrams has never opened the box. To this day, it sits on his desk, that same box, still sealed. "Why have I never opened this? Why have I kept it? I'm not a pack rat," he says. "But, I felt like, somehow, there was a key to this. I realized that I haven't opened it because it represents something important to me … it represents my Grandfather. But it also represents infinite possibility. It represents hope. It represents potential. What I love about this box is that [it helps me] realize that mystery is the catalyst for imagination.

It makes me think that mystery is more important than knowledge … and that's why the Mystery Box—in honor of my grandfather—stays closed."[56]

There's so much wisdom in this statement. In the same way that Abram's imagination about what *could be* inside that box is almost certainly a thousand times better than what is *actually* in that box, our ability to wonder; to be curious, to ask questions, to dream and imagine is more valuable than having all the answers.

Not only this, but when it comes to our curiosity and wonder about who God is and what God is like, the reality is actually *so much better* than anything we could ever hope for, dream of, or imagine. God is like a Magical Mystery Box that sits on the desk of our hearts. We are compelled to wonder about what's inside this marvelous mystery box; to engage our creativity and ask deep questions, all the while knowing that one day, when we spill open this mysterious box at last, what awaits us is more spectacular and joyous than we could possibly fathom.

This, I believe, is why the Apostle Paul wrote these words: "When I came to you, I did not come with eloquence or human wisdom … for I resolved to know nothing while I was with you, except Jesus Christ … " (1 Cor. 2:1-2)

Can we say the same? Are we able to come, not with wisdom, or eloquence, but with humility; admitting that we know nothing except Christ? And even this *knowing* we have is "in part", not the whole. Our *knowing* is something we experience each and every day; as we laugh, and breathe, and enjoy being in this very moment, here and now. Anything else is as foolish as dissecting a bird in search of a song.

---

56 "The Mystery Box", J.J. Abrams, TED Talk, Jan. 14, 2008:
   https://www.youtube.com/watch?v=vpjVgF5JDq8

Without a doubt, there is more of God to know than we will ever know in this life. As the Apostle Paul goes on to remind us " … no eye has seen, no ear has heard, and no human mind has conceived the things God has in store for us."

It may take us a long time to come to this realization, but once we do, we can't unknow it. Because, as Ralph Waldo Emerson said, "The mind, once stretched by a new idea, never returns to its original dimensions."

So, we should be continually transformed by this renewing of our minds. This is why Jesus told us to *metanoia*—"think again." Doubting our answers and questioning our assumptions is how it's supposed to work. The transformation comes as we relax our grip on certainty and plunge deep into the ocean of mystery. We have to let go of one thing to receive what's next. We have to reach the point where we grow tired of caterpillar thinking and begin to enter the cocoon where everything changes.

This process has already begun. We can resist it, or we can embrace it with an open heart. As we fall into the depths of uncertainty, we realize that we are not who we once were, and we are not yet who are becoming. Within the dark unknown of the chrysalis, we allow our imaginations to flow and await the moment of ultimate transformation when we can spread our wings, and fly!

Over the last decade or so, I have changed my mind about so many things. My beliefs about almost everything have shifted. What I've learned about this process is this: *I have been wrong before, and I am probably wrong about something now, and I will, no doubt, be wrong again in the future.*

Being wrong isn't anything to be ashamed of. It's simply the way we make progress on this journey into the deeper mystery of God. My personal identity is not defined by what I believe. It's defined by who

I am; whose image I was created in, and who I am becoming day-by-day as I walk this path; a path marked by unanswered questions and mysterious wonders too great for my mind to fully comprehend.

So, let's hold loosely to our beliefs. Let's practice saying, "I think" or maybe even, "I don't know" when it comes to questions about theology and faith. Let's do our best to become comfortable with our lack of knowledge and learn to embrace the idea that knowing God is closer to falling in love than a lecture behind a pulpit.

What we need so desperately these days is to rediscover a sense of knowing God that allows us to enjoy the experience without feeling the need to define it; to embrace our intimacy with God so that it conceives new life within us, allowing us to become pregnant with a sense of Divine wonder that changes us into people who may be less capable of explaining—but who are more than capable of experiencing—a God who loves us with an everlasting love; a love that is higher, and wider, and longer and deeper, than we could possibly imagine.

In the words of Albert Einstein, "There are only two ways to live your life: One is as though nothing is a miracle. The other is as though everything is a miracle."

I know how I want to live my life.

Do you?

Chapter 9

THE FALSE COMFORT OF KNOWING VS THE INFINITE JOYS OF CHILDLIKE WONDER

"The secret of change is to focus all your energy, not on fighting the old, but on building the new."

SOCRATES

Rather than argue about what people believed about God over 2,000 years ago, let's start here. Right now. Today. What do we *know* of God? What is our *experience* of the Divine? How do we *hear* the voice of Christ today? What is the Eternal, Ever-Present Creator whispering into your heart at this very moment?

With Christ, all things are being made new. So, let's say, "out with the old, and in with the new," and by that we mean the immediate, relevant, up-to-the-nanosecond present reality of our being in the here and now.

If the Kingdom of God is within you, and if it is wide open and available to you and everyone around you, then there's nothing to wait for. There's nothing we lack to begin living and breathing in this exquisite reality of Divine union with God, and everything around us.

If anything, the Universe and all of creation is waiting for you to wake up and begin moving into the deeper awareness of what it means to experience the life of Christ that has always been within you.

Everything you require to accomplish this is within your grasp. Because consciousness itself created reality, and this same consciousness dwells inside of you. Because, as we've seen, matter and energy always respond to consciousness.

The determining factor in all of this is whether or not we are living daily in full awareness of these things. If we are not, then we are allowing our lives to be ruled by our unconscious selves rather than by our conscious awareness. This creates a sort of strange incongruity in our own minds. As Dr. Amit Goswami explains it:

> "This raises the question of what it means to act without awareness—the concept of the unconscious. What is the unconscious in us? The unconscious is that for which there is consciousness but no awareness. Note that there is no paradox here because in the philosophy of idealism consciousness is the ground of being. It is omnipresent, even when we are in an unconscious state ... It is our conscious self that is unconscious of some things most of the time and of everything when we are in dreamless sleep.
>
> "In contrast, the unconscious seems to be conscious of all things all of the time. It never sleeps. That is to say, it is our conscious self that is unconscious of our unconsciousness, and the unconscious that is conscious—we have the two terms backwards ... So, when we speak of unconscious perception, we are speaking of events that we perceive but that we are not aware of perceiving."[57]

Awareness, then, is critical to our shift from unconsciousness to full consciousness. When we can live out of the flow that comes from

---

[57] *The Self-Aware Universe*, by Amit Goswami, pp 108-109

this shift, it's as if we bridge the gap between both the unconscious and the conscious self, so that there is no separation between the two. The reality is that there really is no such thing as separation anyway. Our experience of separation is an illusion that we need to overcome.

Another, less confusing way, to think of this is to realize that the wisdom, and insight and truth we so desperately long for is not "out there" for us to dig up, or discover, or capture like some wild animal hiding in the jungle.

Truth is not external to us. Truth is, and always has been, abiding in us, like Christ in the tomb awaiting the inevitable resurrection.

Now we can see why our old ways of approaching God, and of talking about theology, never worked. Knowing God has never been about having the right information about God. It has always been about knowing and experiencing God's immediate presence in an intimate way.

Hearing God's Voice

So, how do we experience God in the here and now? For some of us, this is an easy question to answer. You may spend time in meditation or silence, or you may encounter God as you spend time in nature, or garden in your back yard, or when you drive in your car, or maybe when you journal your thoughts, or maybe even when you watch a film or read a poem or a book. In those ways, some of us encounter the Divine presence of God. We hear God's voice. We sense God's nearness. We feel God's love. We encounter God in our waking, breathing, everyday experiences.

If that's you, congratulations! You've already found your connection with God and you're experiencing God on a regular basis. As much as possible, I would encourage you to maintain that connection and continue that conversation with God as often as possible.

But, for the rest of you who can honestly say, "I have never heard God's voice, or felt God's presence or experienced God in any of these ways," let me assure you: you are not alone.

I know so many Christians who have grown up in the Church, and attended prayer meetings and worship services and revivals and concerts and sat through thousands of sermons and Bible studies and have never once—as hard as they have tried—heard God or encountered God the way others do.

It took me a while to realize this, I'm embarrassed to admit. For me, the nearness of God and the experience of God has always been there. Even when I was a little boy, and long before my family ever took me to church and before I ever heard the name "Jesus" or walked forward to receive Christ as my Lord and Savior, I have always talked with God, and often I have felt God's response in my heart as I lay there quietly listening.

But, then I discovered, to my surprise, that not everyone had the same experiences I had. That was a shock to me, but now I understand it. We're all wired differently. We're not all the same.

So, if you're one of those who would say "I have never had any experiences with God" or "I've never heard God's voice," I have something I'd like you to consider: Maybe you do hear God's voice, and maybe you do experience God's presence, but you've just not known to call it that.

Here's what I mean: I think sometimes our language concerning our experiences of God get in the way and paint the wrong picture. When I say "God spoke to me" or "I heard the Holy Spirit say …", I don't mean I heard an audible voice. If someone assumed that "hearing God's voice" meant hearing something with their ears, that would be a misunderstanding, and that misunderstanding could prevent someone from realizing what "hearing God's voice" is really like.

My friend Brad Jersak has an excellent response to this problem. What he suggests is that there are several ways that many of us already hear the voice of God in some form or fashion, but we may not think of it that way. As he explains:

"I believe everyone does have an experience of God, but it can get stolen away from us, like the birds that come [in Jesus's Parable of the Sower] and steal away the good seed that is sown on the field. So, we may have an experience but then we say 'that doesn't count' and 'this doesn't count', for whatever reason, and pretty soon nothing counts as an experience with God. If our experiences are too mundane, we dismiss them for not being overly spiritual enough, but if we have an overly spiritual experience we dismiss that because it's just too weird so it must have been our imagination or bad pizza."[58]

Once we stop dismissing everything we experience, we can start to examine some of the ways we do hear from God, and those may not always look the way we expect them to. As Brad continues:

"So, what I like to do is to start with the idea that [as Jesus said], 'I am the Good Shepherd and my sheep hear my voice' and 'If you call on me I will answer.' So, if you are a follower of Christ—one of his sheep—then Christ is capable of speaking to you and making himself heard. If you have ever had any experience of being invited into God's family, what did that feel like? Jesus told us that no one can come to the Father unless the Spirit draws them. So, if you were ever called by God or experienced this invitation, then you've heard God's voice. If it was a moment in time, that counts. If it was a process, then that counts, too. Have you ever read Scripture and felt like anything in there resonated with you? That counts. Have you ever listened to a

---

58 From Square 2, Week 3, "Experiencing Christ": https://www.bk2sq1.com/

pastor or teacher or even a parent or a friend and what they said to you felt like a message? That counts. Is there a hymn, or a chorus or even a song on the radio that speaks to you in some profound way? That counts. If you've ever felt any conviction of sin, that counts. If you've ever felt compassion for another human being and a compulsion to go and help or serve or bless them, that counts. Right there I've listed seven different ways that the Spirit of God is always speaking to us in ways we may not have considered."[59]

Sadly, what often happens is that we tend to downplay or dismiss these sorts of experiences because we've been conditioned to mistrust our own inner voice. We've been told over and over again that we are worms and wretches; that there is nothing good in us, that our thoughts are evil all of the time, and that our hearts are deceitfully wicked and not to be trusted.

So, rather than trust the indwelling Spirit of the Living God within, we are trained to be suspicious of God's voice but to completely trust our human leaders—pastors, preachers and teachers of the Bible—without question. In fact, if you were to doubt or question your spiritual leaders—whom we already know are human like the rest of us and just as prone to get it wrong as anyone else—you would most likely be labeled a heretic and a troublemaker. But doubting the voice of Christ within you is totally okay, and strongly encouraged. What's wrong with this picture?

"That fear has been taught into us," Jersak says. "We've been trained to constantly be on guard for deception, but I find it very weird that we would actually believe that if we would inquire of the Lord we'll

---

be deceived, so if we don't listen to God's voice we're somehow safer. It makes no sense."[60]

When we ask God for bread, we shouldn't expect to receive stones, or scorpions. The God revealed to us by Jesus is a good father who loves to give freely to those who ask.

This fear and doubt that we've been conditioned to accept is intended to prevent us from seeking God directly. Those who perpetuate this myth have a vested interest in making sure you keep coming back to them for answers and wisdom. Once you realize you can hear God's voice yourself, those people are out of a job, or at least their role, position and authority is diminished.

Jesus and the Apostle Paul wanted us to known about the abiding presence of Christ within us, and the Spirit of God that leads us into all truth, and the mind of Christ that we've been given that allows us to question, doubt, reason, consider, and yes, even hear for ourselves the voice of the God who abides within us and makes a home in us.

As we've already pointed out, the Truth is not "out there" but "in here." So, if we can learn to discern God's voice within, then what's preventing us from doing so? Fear, perhaps. Or maybe self-doubt.

Whatever might be keeping you from moving in this direction let me urge you to at least try and hear God's voice. It might take some time. It may involve trying a variety of different activities before you really start to hear something. But one thing I can guarantee you is this: If you never try, you'll never know.

What works for me might not work for you. What works for others, might not work for someone else. But, we should at least consider the possibility that, out of all the inner voices we might hear during the

---

60 Ibid.

day, at least one of those might be the voice of God. So, how can we know which one?

Here's a quick test: If you're sensing an impulse to bless someone else, or to show kindness to a stranger, or to share something, or give something, or speak encouragement to someone, or anything that isn't directly harmful or painful, go with that. Because the Fruits of the Spirit are: Love, Joy, Peace, Patience, Kindness, Gentleness and Self-Control. Anything we suddenly feel or sense in our hearts that pulls us in these directions is most likely from God. And if it's not? You should probably go ahead and do it anyway. Who cares if it's officially from God or not? What matters is loving others as Christ has loved us. If it's our idea, great! That means we're starting to learn to follow Christ without requiring constant instructions to do so. If it's a prompting from God, don't miss your opportunity to bless someone. Either way, our joy is found in doing these things that flow out of our connection with God, who is Love.

Taking Time To Listen

The simplest way that I've found to begin hearing God's voice is to just sit and listen. It may only be for five or ten minutes. But the very act of finding a quiet place, being still, breathing deep, and slowing myself down is usually enough of an opportunity for God to speak. If for no other reason than that I am actually in the posture of listening.

For some of us, the idea of sitting in silence for 5 or 10 minutes can sound like a form of torture. We're sometimes fearful of that silence or of those thoughts. Maybe we've been told that meditation can become some sort of portal to the occult or open us up to demonic influence. Or maybe we're simply the product of a modern Christian culture that has conditioned us to believe that the only way we can experience

God is in a room full of a few hundred others jumping up and down to loud music while surrounded by strobes, colored lights and fog machine ambiance.

All these contradictions aside, the fact is that there have been several hundred of Christian mystics over the last 2,000 years who have encountered God by entering into silent meditation to receive profound spiritual insights that many of us love to quote, without taking the time to seek God in meditation ourselves.

Still others may fear those few minutes of absolute silence simply because we are not sure how to be alone with our thoughts. We may encounter ideas or feelings that we would rather not think about. Or we may simply fear the unknown experiences we may have if we try something so unusual.

The great mystic, Thich Nhat Hanh observed:

"We can spend a lot of time looking for happiness when the world right around us is full of wonder. But our hearts and minds are so full of noise that we can't always hear the call of life and love. To hear that call and respond to it, we need silence … Silence is essential. We need silence, just as much as we need air, and just as much as plants need light. If our minds are crowded with words or thoughts, there is no space for us."[61]

So, as uncomfortable as it might be, we may need to take our need for silence and meditation seriously. Especially if our desire is to draw nearer to the Divine presence and to experience this deeper *ginosko* sense of knowing God.

When we are silent within, we may be astounded at all that we can hear; all the sounds of the world around us, the sighs of nature,

---

61 From the book, *Silence: The Power of Quiet In A World Full Of Noise* by Thich Nhat Hanh, 2016

the rustle of leaves, the songs of birds, the motion of our own breath. All of these sounds surround us on a daily basis, but we are oblivious to them. This creates an unnatural distance between ourselves and nature, or even other people, or our true self.

By listening, we can reconnect with the world around us that is permeated with love, with light, with peace, and with the ever-present reality of Christ in us, and in all things. Our connection with God, and our own incarnation of Christ, is reestablished in that silence. It becomes an oasis for us in a desert of noise and confusion. It resets our inner compass and reorients us toward our true nature and identity as one who is beloved from all eternity and treasured beyond measure by our Abba who is Love.

Physiologically speaking, meditations calms our mind, relaxes our body, reduces our stress levels and activates the pituitary gland which releases oxytocin, dopamine, relaxin, serotonin and endorphins into your bloodstream which brings your entire body and mind into a place of profound peace and well-being.

Why wouldn't we want to take advantage of such an affordable, easily-accessible and beneficial experience?

Rethinking Meditation

Religion is the ultimate expression of dualism. It's what teaches us to look at everything through a binary lens where we can only see good or bad, right or wrong, darkness and light, etc. We are also trained by religion to see ourselves as flawed, defective, broken, or sinful.

Meditation can help us rewire our brains in a way that allows us to take off those binary lenses. It can help us to see ourselves and others, as we really are. My friend Jim Palmer suggests a specific meditation practice for those who are detoxing from religion. It involves cultivating a healthy sense of self-acceptance through the practice of non-attachment. Here's how he explains it:

"As you sit in silence and enter the meditative state, try not to evaluate or respond directly to the feelings and thoughts that arise within you. Our usual response is either attachment or aversion. For example, we may remember something we did during the day and say, 'That was so stupid. How could I be so dumb?' and then this leads us to conclude that we are unlovable, or worthless. Attachment is what leads us to indulge these thoughts and continue reinforcing the feeling until it becomes a deeply held conviction about our identity. Or, we may have a thought that makes us feel guilty and so our impulse is to push that away and dismiss it. That's aversion. Neither one is helpful. Often, our psychological suffering stems from the fact that we either indulge those negative thoughts, or we avoid thoughts we fear might be wrong or sinful.

"So, what I recommend is this: if a thought is unpleasant, don't push it away, and if it's pleasing don't allow it to linger. Just observe your thoughts as they flow into your mind and then allow them to pass out of your mind at their own pace.

"The idea is to set aside some time to sit in silence and allow your mind to become a space of hospitality where thoughts and feelings come and go without any resistance or attachment on your part."[62]

The reason why I think this meditation practice is so helpful is that, for most of us, there's almost no space in our life where we are not prone to judge and condemn ourselves. By allowing our thoughts and feelings to come and go very naturally, we start to realize that there's already an established ebb and flow of our thoughts. We don't need

---

62 From Square 2, week 7, "Silence and Meditation" with Jim Palmer: https://www.bk2sq1.com/

to force thoughts to come, and we don't have to indulge them. The only thing, then, that upsets that natural rhythm is our attachment or aversion. Nothing else.

So, just try this. Take 10 minutes. Quiet yourself. Become a space of hospitality for your thoughts. Whatever occurs during that time; whether fear, anger, stress, anxiety, or whatever, simply allow those to come and go without any kind of judgment, or attachment or resistance.

What you may discover as you go through this a few times is that there is a part of you—who you are—that is bigger than any particular thought or feeling that arises in a given moment. This means: You are not your thoughts. You are not your feelings. Who you are, deep down, is the one who is observing those thoughts and feelings like someone in a movie theater watching actors on the screen.

This meditation not only helps us to recognize that there are always these sorts of thoughts and feelings coming in and out of our minds, but also the realization that you are not your thoughts or your feelings. You are a being who observes all of it from a distance. Those thoughts do not define you, nor should they control you.

What this should also help us to understand is that everything we need for joy, or peace, or fulfillment is already within our grasp. We don't need to chase it down, or earn it, or acquire it somehow. We begin to accept reality as it is. We begin to understand that external things—promotions, fame, money, houses, cars, titles—are not capable of bringing us joy. Joy is already abundantly available within us, like a spring of living water that flows from within. Jesus affirms this truth. The things we strive for do not bring us happiness, and focusing our attention on those things only increases our suffering. But, when we turn our attention to the Kingdom of God, to the indwelling presence of Christ, we find peace that passes understanding and we receive an awareness of the abundance of life within. Consider how Jesus phrases this:

> "Therefore, *I tell you, do not worry about your life, what you will eat or drink; or about your body, what you will wear. Is not life more than food, and the body more than clothes?* Look at the birds of the air; they do not sow or reap or store away in barns, and yet your heavenly Father feeds them. *You are worth more than many sparrows. Can any one of you by worrying add a single hour to your life?*

> "And why do you worry about clothes? See how the flowers of the field grow. They do not labor or spin. Yet I tell you that not even Solomon in all his splendor was dressed like one of these. If that is how God clothes the grass of the field, which is here today and tomorrow is thrown into the fire, will he not much more clothe you—you of little faith? So do not worry, saying, 'What shall we eat?' or 'What shall we drink?' or 'What shall we wear?' For the pagans run after all these things, and your heavenly Father knows that you need them. *But seek first his kingdom and his righteousness, and all these things will be given to you as well.*" (Matthew 6:25-33, emphasis mine)

Simply put, nothing outside of yourself can *make* you happy. Not your spouse, not your success, not even winning the lottery. Those things may provide a temporary boost of excitement, but once this fades you realize something profound: *I am still the same person I was before.*

Happiness is not something out there for you to find. It is something within you that you must discover and realize for yourself.

Meditation can help us to reorient our frequency, like a tuning fork that brings every string into harmony with the tone of heavenly peace.

How Do We Know Truth?

If Truth is not something external to myself, something "out there" to be discovered, or learned from a pastor, or theologian, or guru, or underlined in a book; if truth is within us, accessible to all of us at any time, then how do we know Truth when we see or experience it?

Let's face it. Knowing that Truth is "in here" is not the same as recognizing Truth once we encounter it. How do we evaluate our experiences? How can we be sure that the Truth we think we've discovered is, in fact, the Truth?

The first thing to point out here is that Truth is only something you can know through direct experience. You cannot read it in a book or hear it in a sermon. Not if you want that truth to be your own. In other words, any good teacher or guru will urge you not to take their word for something but to "taste and see" for yourself whether something is true or not. We have to experience truth to know if it's real or not. The guru might say "Meditation will bring you peace and joy," for example. But until you engage in the practice of meditation yourself and experience that peace and joy, you will never know if it's true or not. Knowing the truth—in this case, "Meditation will bring you peace and joy"—is only possible when you experience it directly.

This is why Jesus was so often pointing out to his disciples the gap between knowing something and doing something. After he washed their feet, for example, he emphasized the point of all of it by saying:

> "Now that I, your Lord and Teacher, have washed your feet, you also should wash one another's feet. I have set you an example that you should do as I have done for you. Very truly I tell you, no servant is greater than his master, nor is a messenger greater than the one who sent him. *Now that you know these things, you will be blessed if you do them.*" (John 13:14-17, emphasis mine)

So often we act as if knowing the right information is all that is necessary for us to be blessed. But, here, Jesus contradicts that notion by affirming that it's only when we put what we know into practice that the blessing is received.

Direct experience is one of the main ways we know something is true. If we put what we think we know into practice, we can easily discover if it's true nor not.

Another way for us to determine whether something is true or not is through critical thinking. Religion has cowered many of us into mistrusting this part of our brain. We've been told not to question, not to think logically, not to think critically about what our teachers say to us. But, this resistance to critical thinking is what leads to blind faith. Once we relinquish our God-given ability to think critically about things, we have opened ourselves up to manipulation and control. Christ said the Truth would set us free, not bind us in the chains of ignorance. Thinking for ourselves, and trusting our own ability to discern truth, is essential for spiritual growth and development.

Here are a few examples of where Jesus and the Apostles affirm our freedom to know truth when we see it:

"And I will ask the Father, and *he will give you another advocate to help you and be with you forever—the Spirit of truth.* The world cannot accept him, because it neither sees him nor knows him. *But you know him, for he lives with you and will be in you.*" (John 14:16-17, emphasis mine)

"I have much more to say to you, more than you can now bear. *But when he, the Spirit of truth, comes, he will guide you into all the truth.* He will not speak on his own; *he will speak only what he hears, and he will tell you what is yet to come.* He will glorify me because it is from me that he will receive what *he will make known to you.*" (John 16:12-14, emphasis mine)

"As for you, *the anointing you received from him remains in you, and you do not need anyone to teach you.* But as his anointing teaches you about all things and as that anointing is real, not counterfeit—just as it has taught you, remain in him." (1 John 2:27, emphasis mine)

"*The person with the Spirit makes judgments about all things, but such a person is not subject to human judgments,* for, "Who has known the mind of the Lord so as to instruct him?" *But we have the mind of Christ.*" (1 Corinthians 2:15-16, emphasis mine)

"And *the peace of God, which transcends all understanding, will guard your hearts and your minds* in Christ Jesus." (Philippians 4:7, emphasis mine)

It may come as a shock to some of us that these verses are even in the Bible at all. We've been conditioned for so long to doubt ourselves, mistrust our thoughts, and be suspicious of our own hearts. Yet, the reality is that Jesus trusts us to hear the voice of the Good Shepherd. He believes that we are more than capable of knowing and understanding truth when we see it. Can we have that same confidence for ourselves?

Another way we can know what is true is the process of self-reflection. Meditation can help us greatly in this area. Especially the more comfortable we become sitting in silence and focusing our attention on what's inside rather than constantly being influenced and controlled by what is outside of us.

One final way we can know whether something is true or not is to share it with a trusted companion. These people are gifts from God to us. They can help us to see things we may have missed, identify blind spots we're not aware of, and think about things from a perspective we haven't considered. For me, this person is my wife, Wendy. For you it may be a parent, a best friend, or a mentor. Whoever it may be, if you have someone in your life like this, be sure to take advantage of their wisdom whenever necessary.

This doesn't mean that we elevate this person to the status of guru or spiritual authority in our lives. To do that is to place ourselves back into the mindset that what we need is external to ourselves, or that someone else is more capable of hearing from God or knowing Truth than we are. At the same time, it's always a good idea to run things by those who love us the most; people who have demonstrated an ability to provide insight whenever needed, and always with our best interests in mind.

Asking the opinion of these trusted companions does not relinquish our ability to make the final determination of what is true or not. We are free to listen to their perspective, question their assumptions, and even disagree with their conclusions. The dialog itself is what is most helpful to us as we learn to develop our own ability to discern Truth when we see it.

Overcoming Our Fear

As a reminder, when we talk about learning to identify Truth when we encounter it, we should not allow ourselves to slip back into the old way of thinking that defines our faith as having the right information about God, or that leans on the illusion of certainty about the Divine.

Faith is not about knowing information. It's about admitting that we are in direct connection with a Being of such exceptional splendor that no one could ever possibly know—in an intellectual sense— almost anything at all. God is a mystery to be explored, not a doctrine to be memorized.

This shift away from certainty towards mystery can be uncomfortable and disorienting for many of us. As my friend Kim Cowling explains:

"Becoming more aware of how little we know and how little we can actually be certain of does not feel like growth. In fact, losing the illusions of our past certitudes can feel like the antithesis of growth. It's deeply disorienting and can appear to ourselves, and others, like regression and even something to fear.

"I think this is, in part, because our idea of growth has too often been paired with the idea of accumulating information, techniques and strategies, or other knowledge. So, shedding and releasing all the information, beliefs and habits we've accumulated, that we now realize were unhealthy and unhelpful, tends not to seem like progress at all.

"Recognizing that much of the information and knowledge we possessed was merely constructed to make sense of life at the time (but may not have had a great deal to do with reality) feels like a serious loss.

"Indeed, it is a serious loss. It's deeply painful; emotionally and intellectually devastating, and very socially isolating.

"And it definitely is growth. Unlearning is growth. Paradoxically, unlearning is learning.

"For those who are in the throes of this discombobulating process right now; You are not alone. Also, please keep going! There is life and freedom on the other side of that pain!" [63]

I can't help but feel as if this is exactly what Jesus was urging us to do when he kicked off his Sermon on the Mount by saying, "Rethink everything! The Kingdom of God is here!" (Matthew 3:2)

Unlearning is growth. Letting go is gain. Those who lose their life find it. It's the beautiful paradox of the Kingdom of God within.

---

63 As quoted from a post by Kim Cowling on Facebook, January 26, 2022.

But, learning to let go, and to hold loosely to our beliefs isn't easy. We want answers. We crave certainty. We need absolutes. Or, we used to think we did, at any rate. Hopefully, we're beginning to see the wisdom of not knowing, and the beauty of embracing the mystery, even if we're not completely comfortable stepping into that reality.

Much of our discomfort about shifting away from knowing and abandoning our need to be right is the feeling that the path is unclear. We want guideposts. We want a road map. We want clearly marked signs along the path. But, do we really? Is that essential to our spiritual growth? Or, is faith, by definition, the hope of things not seen? As my friend Jim Palmer once said, "Actually, the only thing you really need is to see the next step. People become paralyzed because they cannot see how it's all going to work out. Just focus on doing the next thing."

That's what it means to walk by faith, isn't it? To trust even when you can't see. To believe even when you aren't sure. To hope even in the darkest night.

Never settle for the false comfort of certainty. It can never compare to the infinite joy and exquisite wonder of the endless mystery of God.

Certainty is an illusion anyway. No one knows anything for sure. What we see, what we hear, what we remember—all of that is permeated with glorious uncertainty. Reality is weirder than we ever imagined.

The best we can do is to let go of our fear, abandon our expertise, and just relax and enjoy the ride.

Chapter 10

STRANGE FREQUENCIES

*"If you want to find the secrets of the universe, think
in terms of energy, frequency and vibration."*

NICOLA TESLA

*"The search for knowledge is not nourished by certainty:
it is nourished by a radical distrust of certainty."*

CARLO ROVELLI[64]

It was in the fall of 1632 that Galileo Galilei first discovered the strange patterns created by sound waves. As he was scraping a brass plate with a sharp iron chisel one day, he began to hear the plate vibrate, creating a high-pitched sound wave with each stroke. Upon closer inspection, he noticed that the flakes of brass on the plate began to form geometric patterns. "Scraping with the chisel over and over again, I noticed that it was only when the plate emitted this noise that any marks were left upon it," he wrote.

A few years later, in July of 1680, English scientist Robert Hooke performed a similar experiment using a violin bow to create vibrations on a glass plate. That experiment formed similar nodal patterns in

---

64 *Reality Is Not What It Seems,* by Carlo Rovelli, pg. 261

grains of salt, revealing distinct geometric patterns that corresponded to specific frequencies.

This research eventually inspired the extensive work of Dr. Hans Jenny who coined the term "Cymatics" in the 1960s to describe this strange phenomenon. His contribution to this field was significant because he documented his findings in dozens of photographs and he eventually filmed the particles responding to sound frequencies in real time so the effect could be seen as it happened.[65]

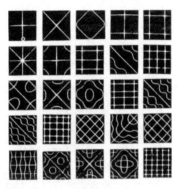

Image: Photographs of sand particles forming geometric shapes in response to sound waves.

Would it surprise you to learn that the sound of the human heartbeat also forms similar geometric patterns? It's true. For some unknown reason, particles respond to sound frequencies by arranging themselves into mathematically precise shapes.

---

65 For more on this phenomenon of how sound creates geometric patterns go here: https://www.thisiscolossal.com/2013/06/ the-visual-patterns-of-audio-frequencies-seen-through-vibrating-sand/

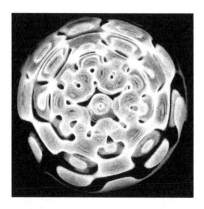

Scientists have also observed this same phenomenon with water in response to harmonic frequencies; creating the same geometric patterns and shapes as found with salt, sand and other particles.

So, what does this all mean? Let's take a moment to consider a few things. If we know that the human body is composed of up to 60 percent water, and the human brain and heart are 73 percent water, and if sound waves create resonant patterns, and if those same patterns are observably present in nature around us, then perhaps this explains the emotional power of music.

Perhaps this is why music can bring us to tears or even release tension and anxiety in our body? Maybe this is why certain songs can change our brain chemistry and alter our moods? It might even explain why music can become a catalyst for so many of us to experience feelings of connection to God and the Universe around us?

Looking Up

Moving from the acoustic realm to the celestial, famed scientist Johannes Kepler observed an idyllic five-fold symmetry in the 1600s when mapping the geocentric motion of the planet Mars in relation to Earth.

What he discovered was an incredibly similar phenomenon taking place in the heavens above us. One that could only be detected through patient observance and mathematical measurement. The results he sketched out were fascinating.

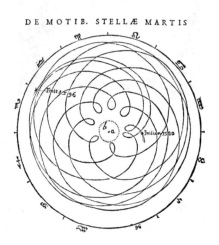

Once again, a mathematically perfect geometric pattern emerged. Using this same method, astronomers were able to map every planet in our solar system. What they found was astonishing: each planet created its own unique geometric signature which was repeated, almost exactly, every 365 days, as observed from earth. Note: These patterns are not observable from space. They only appear when we trace the elliptical orbital patterns of each planet as seen from our own planet. Still, the patterns exist and they are shockingly geometrical and distinct for each planet in relation to our own, as seen in the image below.

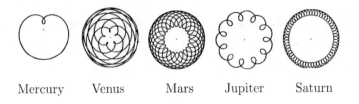

Mercury   Venus   Mars   Jupiter   Saturn

We should also note that these elliptical patterns are formed over varying time frames. For example, Venus takes 8 years to complete its pattern, while Jupiter and Saturn complete their patterns every 20 years.

As Above So Below

Scientists have also noticed strange similarities in the patterns repeated in human biology and the world around us. Is it a coincidence that the bronchial tubes in our lungs resemble the shape of branches in trees? Or that trees create oxygen that we breathe through our lungs which, in turn, creates carbon dioxide that trees and other plants need to survive? Is it merely a coincidence that the neurons in our brain resemble the structure of galaxies in our universe? Or that the blood vessels in our eyes are nearly identical to the veins in leaves? Or that the death of a star in outer space mimics the motion of a cell's birth?

These patterns are repeated across organisms, and appear at the celestial, microscopic and macroscopic levels. Why is this? That is another mystery for us to explore. But, it's clear that our bodies share the same observable patterns that we see embedded within all other living things in our universe.

What's also a little shocking is to realize that our body is a vast ecosystem in itself; home to around 90 trillion microbes living on our body, and millions of bacteria living on us, and inside of us.

Believe it or not, there are as many living organisms on your body right now as there are people on earth.

One tiny creature who lives on your body is the Demodex, an 8-legged microscopic insect that enjoys feasting on your dead skin cells.[66] There are also vast colonies of bacteria that live on your tongue, teeth, skin and inside of your intestines. Some of them are harmful, but most of them are good for you and help aid in digestion or help keep your body healthy. You and I even play host to entire gardens of microscopic fungi that thrive on each of our hair follicles, and we even carry viruses, some of which may linger in our nerve cells, rent free, for several years.

The fact is, while the human body contains nearly 100 Trillion cells, only one in 10 of those cells is actually *human*. The other 90 percent of the cells in your body are bacteria, viruses and other microscopic organisms. So, you really are more than the sum of all your biological parts. As Lisa Proctor of the National Institutes of Health says, "The human we see in the mirror is made up of more microbes than human."[67]

Even more fascinating is what Proctor and other Microbiologists are now discovering about this complex ecosystem that exists in our bodies: *These organisms can actually communicate.* "For example, the microbes in a pregnant woman's birth canal start to change just before she gives birth. Scientists think that's so their babies are born with just the right microbiome they'll need to live long, healthy lives."[68]

---

66 For a better look at these microscopic creatures, watch this: https://www.labroots.com/trending/videos/10270/microscopic-view-of-the-invisible-creatures-living-on-our-bodies/amp

67 Finally, A Map Of All The Microbes On Your Body, Rob Stein, NPR.com, June 13, 2012: https://www.npr.org/sections/health-shots/2012/06/13/154913334/finally-a-map-of-all-the-microbes-on-your-body

68 Ibid.

This symbiotic communication system allows these microbial ecosystems to work in harmony together with our own cells to ensure everything runs smoothly. But why? Perhaps because our bodies are what keep those fragile ecosystems alive. Without us, those trillions of living organisms would cease to exist. Our survival is their survival. Oddly enough, since there are technically more of them than us in this body we share, we're greatly outnumbered. So, in a way, no one cares more about our body's health than they do.

Still, there is another mystery for scientists to solve: "How do they talk to our human cells? And how do human cells talk back to them? It's really a concert that they're playing together, and that's what makes us who we are."[69]

Did someone say, "a concert"? Is there some frequency of sound or chemical reaction going on between our human cells and those trillions of microbes we share this body with? Is there some harmonic resonance our ears cannot detect or some geometric patterns created that we cannot yet measure? Yet another unfathomable mystery for us to consider. Either way, we are each a universe unto ourselves. Multiple billions of living creatures make their homes on our skin and inside our body, without our knowledge.

Do they know who you are? Are they aware of what's beyond their limited microscopic universe?

Are we?

Perhaps we are all just tiny organisms within the larger organism we call the Universe?

What if our Universe is a single cell in the body of a larger being who is in turn a small component of yet another being?

_____

69 Ibid.

Where does it end? No one really knows.

If nothing else, these realizations should lead us to conclude that everything really is connected, and our place in this universe is not accidental, or arbitrary.

Everything matters. Everything belongs.

Universal Patterns

The more we begin to look for these patterns, the more we begin to see them everywhere, in everything, all of the time.

We can hardly escape the testimony of all creation as it reveals the fingerprint of the Divine presence from the microscopic to the macro, and beyond.

What all of this should tell us is that life is embedded with structure and meaning and purpose; that beauty and wonder and connection permeate everything in the Universe. Nothing is untouched by this beauty. Nothing is unmoved by this purpose. Nothing is superfluous in this design.

Not even you.

Yes, you. You matter. You are beautiful. You are necessary. You are infused—inside and out—with the frequency of God.

Love brought you here. Love formed you out of nothing. Love invites you to delight in this wondrous universe that is spilling over with an abundance of awe.

We do not live in a simplistic universe, my friends. Our existence is not marked by bland sameness, or boring predictability.

Every new discovery inspires yet another fascinating series of questions which serve to tantalize us, mystify us, and provoke us to dig deeper, search farther, reach higher than we ever thought possible.

Who has hidden these patterns in our universe? Who has embedded every facet of this universe with untold wonders? Who has infused our reality with such exquisite mystery? Don't you want to know? Aren't you even a little bit curious?

By now we must humbly confess to ourselves that certainty is an illusion, and mystery is the language of reality.

The fabric of the universe and all reality is woven together with threads of infinite mystery. The only way to even begin our wondrous journey into the unknown depths of Divine mystery is to let go of what we think we know.

As physicist Carlo Rovelli explains,

"The universe is multiform and boundless, and we continue to stumble upon new aspects of it. The more we learn about the world, the more we are amazed by its variety, beauty and simplicity … .the more we discover, the more we understand that what we don't know yet is greater than what we know."[70]

Whatever so-called knowledge we now cling to must be abandoned if we hope to encounter the joyous wonders that await us just outside of our comfort zones.

There is more to know than you know. Let the expedition into the great unknown begin!

---

70 *Reality Is Not What It Seems*, Carlo Rovelli, pp. 6

Chapter 11

BE YOUR OWN GURU

"Judge a man by his questions, rather than his answers."
VOLTAIRE

*"If anyone thinks he knows something, he has
not yet known as he ought to know."*
THE APOSTLE PAUL (1 COR. 8:2, DBH)

When I was in my early Twenties, I was licensed and ordained by the Southern Baptist Church where my family and I attended.

By that time, I had already been serving as a volunteer music minister for several years. So, after their previous music pastor passed away, I was officially asked to step into that role. Little did I know what was in store for me once I did.

After only a few months in the position, it became very clear that the woman who was playing the organ every Sunday—my Mom's best friend—was having an affair with our founding pastor—a man who was old enough to be her father.

As shocking and painful as this realization was for all of us, it was especially hurtful for me because I had looked up to this gentleman for so long. He was like a Grandfather to me. I just couldn't believe he would do this. Especially knowing what it would do to her marriage and family, and his own wife and children. Even worse was when the

Deacon board and the pastoral staff [which included me], confronted him about this, he not only didn't deny it, he declared the affair to be "God's Will" and refused to step down, or end the relationship.

Eventually, the two of them left the church. A year later, he was dead from a blood disease and she was back with her husband who had forgiven her and welcomed her with open arms.

This whole ordeal was my first real "trial by fire" as a young Christian minister. I made a lot of mistakes, of course, but the one thing I learned from all of it was simply this: *Never place any pastor, teacher, minister or guru on a pedestal again.*

Over the years I had plenty of opportunities to re-learn this lesson. More leaders turned out to be charlatans, manipulators and abusers than I would have ever imagined. Very quickly I realized that preaching about Jesus doesn't guarantee a life that reflects the character of Jesus. That's true of everyone, including myself.

Perhaps this is why I've found it so easy to let go of the notion that anyone needs a spiritual guru to find truth or follow Christ. Loving God and loving others is a fairly simple philosophy, at least in theory. And I don't need anyone to tell me what to believe or how to follow Jesus. Neither do you.

As we've seen, both Jesus and the Apostle Paul affirm our ability to know what's true apart from any teacher, or leader, or pastor, or guru:

The Spirit of Truth has been poured out on all flesh.[71]

We have all received an anointing—the same as Christ—that is real, and remains, and will not fade away; that teaches us about all things and reveals the truth to all of us.[72]

---

71 Acts 2:1-18

72 1 John 2:20; 27

We have been given the mind of Christ, which allows us to question, and doubt, and ponder, and to seek and find what is true.[73]

We have all been filled with the fullness of Christ who fills everything in every way.[74]

We have all been given everything we need to live a Godly life.[75]

We are all in Christ, who is in the Father, and the Father is in him.[76]

We all abide in Christ, who abides in us and makes his home in us.[77]

We are all created in the image of God, who is love, and all who live in love live in God, and God lives in us.[78]

So, none of us needs anyone else to show us who God is. None of us needs anyone to tell us what the Truth is, because we can all know God directly, and we can all know the Truth for ourselves. This is, in fact, what the New Covenant is all about.

See for yourself:

> [10] *This is the [new] covenant I will establish with the people of Israel*
> *after that time, declares the Lord.*
> *I will put my laws in their minds*
> *and write them on their hearts.*
> *I will be their God,*
> *and they will be my people.*

---

73 1 Corinthians 2:16

74 Ephesians 1:23

75 2 Peter 1:3-11

76 John 14:20

77 John 14:23; 15:4

78 1 John 4:16

[11] No longer will they teach their neighbor,
  or say to one another, 'Know the Lord,'
because they will all know me,
  from the least of them to the greatest.
[12] For I will forgive their wickedness
  and will remember their sins no more."
[13] By calling this covenant "new," he has made the first one obsolete; and
what is obsolete and outdated will soon disappear." (Hebrews 8:10-13,
emphasis mine)

The New Covenant—which Jesus initiated with his disciples in the
Upper Room the night before he was crucified—is now in effect. We
affirm this New Covenant every time we share Communion together,
signifying that God has written his laws [summarized by Jesus as "to
love God and love your neighbor as yourself"] in our hearts, and that
no one needs to "teach their neighbor" about God because we can all
know God ourselves—from the least to the greatest.

If we believe this, then it means that we have no need for experts,
for gurus, or pastors or Bible teachers. We all have a direct line to
God by the power of the indwelling Holy Spirit of Christ that abides
within all of us.

Now, this doesn't mean we can't learn something from another
person. Of course, we can all benefit from the wisdom of other
teachers. But what it does mean is that none of us should ever hand
off responsibility for knowing the Truth for ourselves.

There's a big difference between listening to a teacher or learning
from a sermon, and blindly following or accepting anything and
everything a teacher says without question. We get into trouble
whenever we take one person's perspective and adopt it as our own
without utilizing our own God-given ability to discern Truth directly
from the Source.

Not only is this a direct contradiction of the New Covenant that Jesus shed his blood to initiate, it's also a denial of our own God-given birthright as the Children of God who have been given the ultimate gift: the indwelling life and Spirit of Christ within!

Why would we ever accept any substitute? What on earth would ever posses us to trust the words of another person rather than develop our own ability to hear directly from the Creator of the Universe who has come to abide within and make a home in us?

Perhaps we mistrust our own ability to know the Truth. Maybe we're afraid of getting it wrong? But, if we're honest, the Christian Church, led by Christian leaders through the ages has gotten it wrong on almost everything: Slavery, Patriarchy, Genocide, Sexuality, Nationalism, Tribalism, Xenophobia, Torture, etc.

I'm not saying we'll never get it wrong if we learn to listen to the voice of the Good Shepherd who dwells within us. Humanity's ability to get it wrong seems nearly inexhaustible, to be honest. So, of course we're liable to get it wrong now and again. But, what I *am* saying is that listening to the voice of the Holy Spirit is our best chance to get it right.

So much of what we've been told is wrong anyway. As we're learning, much of the theology we were taught wasn't the whole story. We've had to question and doubt and deconstruct almost everything we were taught to believe by those very same pastors, teachers and leaders we allowed to think for us. Why continue to let someone else tell us what's true when we're all capable of finding and knowing the Truth for ourselves?

Our old ways of thinking and knowing led us into more darkness, away from the Light of Truth that was always shining brightly within us. We cannot afford to allow other people to think for us, or to tell us what to believe.

In the first great Reformation of the Christian faith, Martin Luther asserted that everyone should be allowed to read the scriptures for themselves rather than continue to be subjected to the interpretations of the Catholic Church. Today, I believe we need another Reformation that allows every follower of Christ to become their own spiritual guru rather than continue to be subjected to the rule of their pastors, or their denominational statement of faith.

Knowing God was never about having all the answers. It has always been about relationship, connection, and experiences with the Divine.

Our senses are inadequate. Our memories are unreliable. Our own brains are incapable of knowing reality as it truly is. Everything we have placed our trust in, to this point, is powerless to help us see what's true and what is not.

"Be still and know" is perhaps the deepest wisdom we have yet to practice.

When we silence the noise, slow our breathing, calm our minds, and listen quietly, we can hear the still, small voice that whispers within us: *"I am with you. You are loved. Rest in me."*

When I slow down, and still myself, and reconnect with Christ within, I find in that silence a deeper wisdom, and a truer peace, and more profound truth than anything I have ever known before.

When I sit in the silence, I realize that the Truth really is "in here" and not "out there." I experience the presence of Christ who truly abides in me as I abide in Christ.

I must admit, as an author, and a teacher, it can sometimes be challenging to know how to share all that God is teaching me in this way. How do I illustrate all the "nothing" that I have come to know? How can I express to you how little I know about God's Spirit or how God speaks to us? How do I share these thoughts and feelings with people who may relinquish control of their own spiritual journey to me, as if I were their guru?

I honestly don't know.

But perhaps this leaves room for God to do more than I expect, more than I imagine, more than I can anticipate.

See, I'm used to dispensing the truth. I've spent a long time creating the illusion that I have all the answers. But, I'm tired of pretending. The truth is, what I know about God is very little. That's why I honestly urge you not to make me your guru. Or anyone else.

I know, people still want a guru. They want a wise teacher who will give them the answers, guide their steps, show them the path.

But the longer people follow someone else, the less ability they will have to hear that voice of Christ within themselves.

So, if I can do anything it would be to point everyone to that eternal connection they already have with God at this very moment.

Learn to be still.

Learn to listen.

Learn to trust your own ability to hear that voice for yourself.

Don't keep asking others for advice.

Stop following me, or anyone else.

You all have an inner guru living inside.

You have the Spirit of Christ abiding within.

Until you connect with this wisdom, listen to this voice, and abide in this Christ, you will never be at peace with yourself, and you'll always be tossed back and forth by this teaching, or that doctrine, or some other leader.

The truth you seek is already available to you.

You just have to listen.

Give it a try and see.

I think you might be surprised.

Chapter 12

MYSTERIUM

"How you get there determines where you will arrive — and what you arrive as ... You cannot give people the conclusions without walking the journey, or they will substitute the conclusions for the journey itself."

RICHARD ROHR, CHRISTIAN MYSTIC

"To accept uncertainty doesn't detract from our sense of mystery. On the contrary, we are immersed in the mystery and the beauty of the world. The world is more extraordinary and profound than any of the fables told by our forefathers. I want to go and see it."

CARLO ROVELLI, THEORETICAL PHYSICIST[79]

Psychologist Dacher Keltner from the University of California at Berkeley, has spent years studying the beneficial effects of wonder and awe on our physical, mental and emotional well-being. Here's what he's learned about developing our sense of mystery:

"It makes us curious rather than judgmental. It makes us collaborative. It makes us humble, sharing and altruistic. It quiets the ego so that you're not thinking about yourself as much."[80]

---

[79] *Reality Is Not What It Seems,* by Carlo Rovelli, pg. 263

[80] From the article "Awe Might Be Our Most Undervalued Emotion. Here's How To Help Children Find It." by Deborah Farmer Kris, *The*

Dr. Keltner also found that shifting our brains into curiosity mode also calms the brain's default network and has been shown to reduce inflammation. "In other words," he says, "don't underestimate the power of goose bumps."[81]

According to Keltner's Research, finding awe isn't as difficult to cultivate as we might think. It just takes intention. "How do you find awe? You allow for unstructured time," Keltner says. "You wander. You drift through. You take a walk with no aim. You slow things down. You allow for mystery and open questions rather than test-driven answers. You allow people to engage in the humanities of dance and visual art and music."[82]

Feeling awe is something we can experience just about anywhere. Spending time in nature, or listening to music, creating art, spending time with friends, all of these activities stimulate our sense of awe and wonder. But, surprisingly, one of the greatest catalysts for awe is the goodness of other people. "It's kindness and courage," says Keltner. "We really have this capacity to be moved by other people."[83]

So, nurturing and cultivating our ability to experience wonder and awe is directly related to our emotional, mental and spiritual well-being. It's available to us simply by slowing down, being still, experiencing the moment, breathing deep, paying attention, appreciating other people, and expressing gratitude for things both large and small.

Washington Post, Nov. 30, 2021: https://www.washingtonpost.com/lifestyle/on-parenting/children-awe-emotion/2021/11/29/0f78a4b0-4c8e-11ec-b0b0-766bbbe79347_story.html?fbclid=IwAR2Klu6foWn-MZ16jBuR3pBC48g91w1nCtCvnlUjId82ycW1UkxaxWJak0c

81 Ibid.

82 Ibid.

83 Ibid.

How do you inspire yourself to embrace the unknown? What compels you to resist the temptation of certainty? Where do you go to refresh your soul in the beautiful mystery of God?

Small Totems

I have started to keep a handful of items with me, or around my office, that keep me grounded in the reality of wonder and remind me of why embracing mystery is so essential.

- My Dad's old Zippo lighter.

- A small bottle of sand with a tiny seashell inside that my wife Wendy gave to me when we were first married.

- Two drawings my sons made for me when they were younger.

- An old black and white photo of my Grandfather as a young boy that looks exactly like me.

- A ticket stub to an Elvis concert I attended with my parents in San Antonio, Texas as a young boy, shortly before he died.

- A police whistle that my Dad used to keep by our telephone to discourage telemarketers.

- An old poster from college that says, "Sometimes well-formed questions are more useful than well-formed answers."

What are the things that remind you of fascination, awe or wonder? Do keep a watch or a ring that belonged to one of your parents? Or a lock of hair from your child? Do you have some reminder of your own childhood? Or a photograph of someone you wish you could hold again? Whatever it is, I'm sure it's something you treasure; something you look at now and again for comfort or joy; something that unlocks a flood of emotions that fill your soul and give you strength and courage when you need it most.

Cultivating awe is a great thing to do with your time. Taking walks on the beach, or even around the block, can put you into the mode of experiencing wonder. Practicing gratitude can shift your brain chemistry and rewire your mind for joy. Spending time in nature, or gardening in your back yard allows your body to absorb sunlight, your lungs to breathe fresh air, and your brain to become stimulated with all of the beauty that surrounds us.

Taking the time to just be in the present moment is so necessary. Learning to be still, and to know that God is near and that we are loved with a love that transcends time, space, and all human comprehension; this is what reminds us of our true self; our true identity as the beloved children of God.

Knowing God is about so much more than gathering information. For most of us, if we stopped learning now, we wouldn't live long enough to put into practice all that we already know. And that's the point, isn't it? The information we have is of no use to us if all we do is hold it in our memory banks. Until we actually step out and put these things into practice, what good are they to us, or to anyone else?

Learning to love and to be loved is what we are here for. It's who we are. It's why we exist. Rather than trying to find the meaning of life, why not simply find what makes our life meaningful and do that? Isn't that what every loving parent wants for their child? To be happy in all they do; to find joy in the life they're living, to bring joy to others around them, and to explore this world—this universe—of unfolding wonder with a heart full of curiosity and an endless capacity for giving and receiving love.

I believe the God who is love wants this for you, too. I believe we were created to ask, seek, knock, and wonder about the world around us, the Divine Presence within us, and the fascinating universe that surrounds us.

I believe God is bigger, and more mysterious, and more fascinating, and more wonderful than any of us could possibly imagine.

I believe the proper approach to such an endlessly remarkable Being is one of quiet awe and reverent curiosity rather than dogmatic knowing or confident certainty.

Our surrender to the vast unknown magnificence of the Divine might sound like this:

> "Your brightness is my darkness. I know nothing of You and, by myself, I cannot even imagine how to go about knowing You. If I imagine you, I am mistaken. If I understand you, I am deluded. If I am conscious and certain I know you, I am crazy. The darkness is enough." [84]

True wisdom is to know that what you know is nothing. True theology is to confess that our knowledge of God is closer to breathing than it is to acquiring information.

If we cannot be certain about nature, or science, or our own memories, or what we see, or what we hear, or what we experience, then we most certainly cannot believe that we could ever be certain about a God so infinitely above and beyond ourselves.

What's even more beautiful is that this mystery leads us into a deeper love and connection with the Divine. These unanswered questions are what draw us nearer. This unquenchable desire to know

---

[84] Thomas Merton, *Dialogues with Silence: Prayers and Drawings*, 2001

and be known is what fuels our yearning, even as we learn to rest in the One who loves us with an everlasting love.

It is here we realize that we have been knitted together in the secret place to be in relational mystery with God and that "in the very mystery of who [we] are, and the very mystery of who God is, we are already intertwined ... "[85]

What more can we do than to embrace such a beautiful mystery?

So, I hope you can find the grace to allow yourself permission to remain awed by those unanswered questions, to hold loosely to the things you think you know, and to become more open to the joy of uncertainty as you celebrate the exquisite beauty of this Divine mystery.

Who knows where this curiosity will take you?

Only you—and God—can say what's next.

This is your next big adventure. This is the great unknown that awaits you.

This is the *Sola Mysterium*.

---

[85] As quoted from Richard Rohr's Daily Meditation: "You and God are Already One", Feb. 25, 2022.

For more information about Keith Giles

or to contact him for speaking engagements,

please visit *www.KeithGiles.com*

Many voices. One message.

Quoir is a boutique publisher
with a singular message: Christ is all.
Venture beyond your boundaries to discover Christ
in ways you never thought possible.

For more information, please visit
www.quoir.com

HERETIC HAPPY HOUR

Burning questions, not people.

Heretic Happy Hour is an unapologetically irreverent, crass, and sometimes profound conversation about the Christian faith. Hosts, Keith Giles, Katy Valentine, Derrick Day, and Matthew Distefano pull no punches and leave no stones unturned. For some serious sacred cow-tipping, there's nothing better than spending an hour of your time with us.

www.heretichappyhour.com

CPSIA information can be obtained
at www.ICGtesting.com
Printed in the USA
BVHW091802240622
640596BV00012B/292